NAMASTE'
SOBER

Paula P.

BALBOA.PRESS

A DIVISION OF HAY HOUSE

Balboa Press books may be ordered through booksellers or by contacting:

Balboa Press
A Division of Hay House
1663 Liberty Drive
Bloomington, IN 47403
www.balboapress.com
844-682-1282

Print information available on the last page.

ISBN: 979-8-7652-3545-4 (sc)
ISBN: 979-8-7652-3546-1 (e)

Balboa Press rev. date: 11/22/2022

Namaste' Sober
Reviews

Meditation is a tremendous help in any recovery or healing process. Many people are intimidated by it and feel that they cannot meditate or quiet their mind. The author has brought together the 12 steps and meditation to help on the recovery path. These meditation scripts are a great tool for those who want to take their 12 step work a little deeper.

Namaste'
Laura Chiusano LCSW, CASAC, CHT.

In this world of challenging life situations, having access to truly effective tools and guidance is needed more than ever. For the hundreds of thousands individuals who are involved in the 12 Step program for recovery comes a **New Effective** way of anchoring in the deeply rooted messages, with a **Series of Guided Meditations** specific to each step.

The author has wonderfully created an easy to integrate step by step process to maximize the participants results.

This is a perfect support mechanism to anyone who chooses to enhance their personal recovery journey.

Highly recommended!

Stephen C. Interrante
Mindfulness Meditation Coach
Certified Consulting Hypnotist

Contents

Part Three
Personal Growth

PART ONE

✳

The 12 Steps

Meditation for Step One

Step One: "We admitted we were powerless over alcohol and our lives had become unmanageable."[1]

"Surrender is the key to ascending and truly transforming your life. Surrender in each moment as it comes, and you will live a life full of rich moments." (Author Unknown)

This meditation starts with a body scan that assists in relaxation and focus and leads into the portion specific on Step One.

- ## *Body Scan*

Now close your eyes… leave all your worries at the door. Allow yourself to relax into the moment. There is only right here, right now.

Clinging to nothing, just be at rest with what is.
(pause)

Focus on your breathing and the words you hear and if your mind gets distracted, let my voice bring you back and then focus again on your breathing.

---

[1] Alcoholics Anonymous Big Book (4th ed.). (2002). Alcoholics Anonymous World Services (Page 59)

Relax now and just breathe.
(pause)

Observe the natural rhythm and flow of your breath.

Take a few moments now, to pay closer attention to it, giving thanks for its presence.
(pause)

Notice the pause at the top of your inhale and again at the bottom of your exhale.
(pause)

Go within, don't think, just breathe.
(pause)

Take a long slow deep breath in and hold it for a moment. Then slowly exhale with a sigh. Allow any tension to melt away.
(pause)

Feel the coolness of the air on the tip of your nose as you inhale and the warmth of the breath as you exhale.
(pause)

Feel the rise of your chest and abdomen on each inhale and the fall on every exhale. As you exhale, let go of any stress or tension, see it floating away, as you gradually relax more deeply with each breath.
(pause)

Grounding ourselves helps us to shed any feelings of anxiety, restlessness, or fear that may be lingering in body or mind.

So, take a few minutes now to feel grounded and simply connected to the earth. Notice the breath as it nourishes every cell of your body.
(pause)

Focused breathing allows your mind to slow down. On your own really focus on your next three breathes as you gently inhale and exhale.
(pause)

Feel the energy that comes from the earth, its strength and stability. Let this energy ground you. Feel that energy come through the souls of your feet, like a breeze flowing through and over your entire body.
(pause)

Now, feeling that grounded energy, begin to feel a tingle in the tips of your toes and the souls of your feet, know that you are safe, stable, supported and loved.
(pause)

Now, gently bring your focus to your ankles, your calves, your thighs, feeling those muscles relax, as you feel yourself sinking into the surface you are resting upon.
(pause)

Breathe in and breathe out.

Move your focus to your buttocks... and hips, release any tension you may be feeling and allow yourself to drift into a state of deep relaxation.

(pause)

Focus on the base of your spine, relaxing the muscles in your lower back, feel a warmth and think of the strong color red, as this area represents stability, safety, and security.

(pause)

Now allow that feeling of warmth and relaxation to move to your lower abdominal muscles, just below your belly button, and think of the warm color orange, as this area represents creativity and sexual energies.

(pause)

Feel your body relaxing with each breathe you take.

(pause)

Move your focus to your upper abdominal muscles, just above your belly button, relax those muscles and feel a warmth and relaxation as you think of the vibrant color yellow, as this area represents will-power, self-esteem, pleasure, and personal responsibility.

(pause)

Breathe in God's love and peace and breathe out all resistance.

(pause)

Now feel the warmth and relaxation move slowly and gently to your heart center, in the middle of your chest

and about two inches in, and think of a beautiful color of green, as this area represents self-love, our love for others and governs our relationships.

(pause)

Feel yourself becoming deeper and deeper relaxed, your breath will assist you.

(pause)

Feel the muscles in your upper back and chest release and open. Relax your neck and shoulders and allow the relaxation to flow through your arms, and hands.

Begin to feel a tingle in your fingertips and allow any remaining tension in your body to flow out through your fingertips and be released into nothingness.

(pause)

Slowly move your focus to your throat, feeling the muscles of your throat loosen and open, as you think of the soft color of light blue, as this area represents the ability to speak clearly and effectively.

Unclench your teeth, release your jaw muscles, relax the muscles in your cheeks, and just breathe.

(pause)

Let your focus move to your eyes. Now, relax your eye lids and your eye sockets.

(pause)

Gently, move your focus to the spot near the middle of your forehead, between your eyebrows. Relax your eyebrows and all the muscles in your forehead, and think of the color indigo blue, as this area represents foresight, intuition, clarity, and is driven by openness and imagination.
(pause)

Bring your focus to the very top of your head, the crown of your head, feel a tingle there as you relax the muscles in your scalp, and feel it opening as you think of the majestic color of purple, as this area represents Divine connection, and a higher state of consciousness.
(pause)

Now, imagine a bright and beautiful ribbon of crystalline white light coming from above and tethering you to the heavens. Let that light flow to you and through you, enveloping you in a bubble of love and protection.
(pause)

Take a deep breath in and as you exhale allow any remaining tension to be released from your body. Repeating these words in your mind, "peace begins within, peace begins within."
(pause)

Just breathe and go within.
(pause)

• *Guided Meditation*

Imagine now that you are in a cottage. You have decided to go on a leisurely walk. As you walk you take in the beauty that surrounds. You are in a beautiful place, without a care in the world. It is the perfect temperature, and you can feel a gentle breeze as you are walking. You see in the distance a hammock and start to walk in that direction. It is a beautiful day and you have found the perfect spot to relax and take a nap. You easily get settled into the hammock and relax in the peacefulness of the moment. You slowly feel yourself drifting off to an easy gentle sleep.
(pause)

As you sleep, you begin to dream. In your dream, you become an observer of various moments in your life. As the observer, you do not have to feel the feelings, you can rise above and see yourself in these moment as if you are watching a scene from a movie.

The first scene is of a time that you have been drinking or using and are now alone and wishing you had not behaved in a certain way or said the things you did. You know what you said and did were wrong, but you just keep repeating the same behavior, again and again. You have come to realize that you are powerless over alcohol, and you know you are ready to do whatever it takes to change.
(pause)

Now, the movie has moved forward to a recent time that you came to realize that you were tired of the unmanageability of your life. Sometimes, you pretend that you are in control, but in your heart, you know that it is just an act. You feel empty inside and know that there must be a better way of living. You are tired of the struggle.

(pause)

The next scene is of people in your life that are possibly hurt and confused. They do not understand what you are feeling or what you are going through, and they do not know how to help. You see how things you have done or said has left wreckage behind. There is anger and regrets.

(pause)

In the next scene, the movie is ending, and you see yourself walking down a wide path, it is obvious many have walked this path before you. As you continue walking, you see others joining you as you trudge down this path, and you know you are not alone. There are signs along the path to guide you on your way and as the movie fades to black you feel yourself breathing a little easier. You know there is work to be done and you are heading in the right direction, putting one foot in front of the other as you take the first step towards a new freedom and a new happiness.

(pause)

Again, you begin to feel the gentle breeze as you awaken from your sleep. You are feeling relaxed and refreshed and you feel a smile slowly growing on your face. As you rise from the hammock, you take a deep breath in as you look around and enjoy the beauty that surrounds you. You are rejuvenated and have a new feeling of confidence about you. You realize as make your way back to the cottage that you are ready to take the next right step.

(pause)

• *Closing*

Start to deepen your breath now and become more aware of your physical body. Take a deep breath in and release it with a sigh. Start to wiggle your fingers and toes, stretch your arms and legs, open your eyes, and come back to the present time and space.

NAMASTE'

Meditation for Step Two

Step Two: "Came to believe that a Power greater than our-selves could restore us to sanity." [2]

"Surrender is the key to ascending and truly transforming your life. Surrender in each moment as it comes, and you will live a life full of rich moments." (Author Unknown)

This meditation starts with a body scan that assists in relaxation and focus and leads into the portion specific on Step Two.

• *Body Scan*

Now close your eyes... leave all your worries at the door. Allow yourself to relax into the moment. There is only right here, right now.

Clinging to nothing, just be at rest with what is.
(pause)

Focus on your breathing and the words you hear and if your mind gets distracted, let my voice bring you back and then focus again on your breathing.

---

[2] Alcoholics Anonymous Big Book (4th ed.). (2002). Alcoholics Anonymous World Services (Page 59)

Relax now and just breathe.
(pause)

Observe the natural rhythm and flow of your breath.

Take a few moments now, to pay closer attention to it, giving thanks for its presence.
(pause)

Notice the pause at the top of your inhale and again at the bottom of your exhale.
(pause)

Go within, don't think, just breathe.
(pause)

Take a long slow deep breath in and hold it for a moment. Then slowly exhale with a sigh. Allow any tension to melt away.
(pause)

Feel the coolness of the air on the tip of your nose as you inhale and the warmth of the breath as you exhale.
(pause)

Feel the rise of your chest and abdomen on each inhale and the fall on every exhale. As you exhale, let go of any stress or tension, see it floating away, as you gradually relax more deeply with each breath.
(pause)

Grounding ourselves helps us to shed any feelings of anxiety, restlessness, or fear that may be lingering in body or mind.

So, take a few minutes now to feel grounded and simply connected to the earth. Notice the breath as it nourishes every cell of your body.
(pause)

Focused breathing allows your mind to slow down. On your own really focus on your next three breathes as you gently inhale and exhale.
(pause)

Feel the energy that comes from the earth, its strength and stability. Let this energy ground you. Feel that energy come through the souls of your feet, like a breeze flowing through and over your entire body.
(pause)

Now, feeling that grounded energy, begin to feel a tingle in the tips of your toes and the souls of your feet, know that you are safe, stable, supported and loved.
(pause)

Now, gently bring your focus to your ankles, your calves, your thighs, feeling those muscles relax, as you feel yourself sinking into the surface you are resting upon.
(pause)

Breathe in and breathe out.

Move your focus to your buttocks... and hips, release any tension you may be feeling and allow yourself to drift into a state of deep relaxation.

(pause)

Focus on the base of your spine, relaxing the muscles in your lower back, feel a warmth and think of the strong color red, as this area represents stability, safety, and security.

(pause)

Now allow that feeling of warmth and relaxation to move to your lower abdominal muscles, just below your belly button, and think of the warm color orange, as this area represents creativity and sexual energies.

(pause)

Feel your body relaxing with each breath you take.

(pause)

Move your focus to your upper abdominal muscles, just above your belly button, relax those muscles and feel a warmth and relaxation as you think of the vibrant color yellow, as this area represents will-power, self-esteem, pleasure, and personal responsibility.

(pause)

Breathe in God's love and peace and breathe out all resistance.

(pause)

Now feel the warmth and relaxation move slowly and gently to your heart center, in the middle of your chest

and about two inches in, and think of a beautiful color of green, as this area represents self-love, our love for others and governs our relationships.

(pause)

Feel yourself becoming deeper and deeper relaxed, your breath will assist you.

(pause)

Feel the muscles in your upper back and chest release and open. Relax your neck and shoulders and allow the relaxation to flow through your arms, and hands.

Begin to feel a tingle in your fingertips and allow any remaining tension in your body to flow out through your fingertips and be released into nothingness.

(pause)

Slowly move your focus to your throat, feeling the muscles of your throat loosen and open, as you think of the soft color of light blue, as this area represents the ability to speak clearly and effectively.

Unclench your teeth, release your jaw muscles, relax the muscles in your cheeks, and just breathe.

(pause)

Let your focus move to your eyes. Now, relax your eye lids and your eye sockets.

(pause)

Gently, move your focus to the spot near the middle of your forehead, between your eyebrows. Relax your eyebrows and all the muscles in your forehead, and think of the color indigo blue, as this area represents foresight, intuition, clarity, and is driven by openness and imagination.
(pause)

Bring your focus to the very top of your head, the crown of your head, feel a tingle there as you relax the muscles in your scalp, and feel it opening as you think of the majestic color of purple, as this area represents Divine connection, and a higher state of consciousness.
(pause)

Now, imagine a bright and beautiful ribbon of crystalline white light coming from above and tethering you to the heavens. Let that light flow to you and through you, enveloping you in a bubble of love and protection.
(pause)

Take a deep breath in and as you exhale allow any remaining tension to be released from your body. Repeating these words in your mind, "peace begins within, peace begins within."
(pause)

Just breathe and go within.
(pause)

• *Guided Meditation*

What is sanity[3]? The definition says, "Soundness of Mind". In Step One, "We admitted we were powerless over alcohol and our lives had become unmanageable."[4] None of us come to recovery on a winning streak. We had some stinking thinking. As well as repeating behaviors we wished we could stop. With that in mind, we could see the insanity of our lives. If we could make these changes ourselves, we would have, so we admitted we needed help.

Just where does that help come from? It must come from a Power Greater than Ourselves. Just what that looks like varies for each of us, so for now, all you truly need is an open mind and a willingness to listen to how others, "Came to Believe."
(pause)

Take a deep breath in and exhale with a big sigh. Relax, and listen with an open mind as this meditation shares with you, thoughts, and ideas of how many others have found a Power Greater than themselves as they reached out for help and walked down the wide path, the same path that is before you. Remember, as you trudge down this path, that you are not alone.
(pause)

---

[3] *Merriam-Webster.com Dictionary*, Merriam-Webster, https://www.merriam-webster.com/dictionary/sanity. Accessed 12 Aug. 2022.
[4] Alcoholics Anonymous Big Book (4th ed.). (2002). Alcoholics Anonymous World Services (Page 59)

What a Higher Power looks like can vary in many ways. Here are some examples; Source Energy, Creator of the Universe, the Power of a Group of Drunks (G.O.D.), Gift of Desperation (G.O.D.) or perhaps just some Good Orderly Direction (G.O.D.) some may believe in "God" in a religious reference. It is an individual journey.

(pause)

Some who were uncomfortable with the GOD idea, were suggested to borrow their sponsors GOD until they found the GOD of their understanding.

(pause)

How can a Group of Drunks be GOD? When you witness how others have changed their lives, perhaps you will come to believe that you can as well.

What Good Orderly Direction could be GOD? Following the suggestions/directions of your sponsor, attending meetings, reading the Big Book of Alcoholics, and working the 12 steps can lead you to be able to do something you could not do by yourself.

(pause)

Each of us has come to believe in a Power Greater than Ourselves. It does not need to be religious. It is a Spiritual connection to something bigger than ourselves. There are no rules and when you are honest, being open minded and willing, you will discover a God of your own understanding.

(pause)

Take this moment to imagine a time when you were desperate for help, and you called out to God, if there really is a God out there! What were you in need of; guidance, protection, saving from a situation, wisdom, peace, maybe courage?
(pause)

Think back and remember, how you felt, were you desperate? Did you feel like perhaps there was something out there bigger than yourself that could help you?
(pause)

Even if that hope or belief was just as small as a mustard seed, did you feel it? That belief is what is needed for a beginning.
(pause)

You are tired and ready to let go and allow someone or something else carry the load. You know you are ready to do whatever it takes to change. Right now, recognizing that perhaps there is a better way, is good start.
(pause)

There are family members or friends in your life that would help if they had the power and knew how, but they don't. There is one is who has all power, that one is God.

Breathe easy, knowing that you have come to believe that a Power Greater than yourself could restore you to sanity.
(pause)

As you continue walking this wide path, there are still others joining you. Feel that safety in knowing that you are not alone. There is a hope in your heart now that you have come to be open and willing to believe, that there is a Power Greater than yourself. You can feel yourself breathing a little easier knowing that you can let go of trying to control everything.
(pause)

Now take a deep breath in and exhale. Again, focus on your breathing. Feeling your lungs expand on each inhale and relax on each exhale. Take three deep breaths in and out on your own now.
(pause)

Now relax and let your breathing fall back into a gentle natural rhythm.
(pause)

Don't think, just breathe
(pause)

You may be feeling rejuvenated and have a new feeling of confidence about you. There is more work to be done and you are heading in the right direction, putting one foot in front of the other as you take the second step towards a new freedom and a new happiness.
(pause)

You know you are ready to take the next right step.
(pause)

• *Closing*

Start to deepen your breath now and become more aware of your physical body. Take a deep breath in and release it with a sigh. Start to wiggle your fingers and toes, stretch your arms and legs, open your eyes, and come back to the present time and space.

NAMASTE'

Meditation for Step Three

Step Three: "Made a decision to turn our will and our lives over to the care of God as we understood Him"[5]

"Surrender is the key to ascending and truly transforming your life. Surrender in each moment as it comes, and you will live a life full of rich moments." (Author Unknown)

This meditation starts with a body scan that assists in relaxation and focus and leads into the portion specific on Step Three.

• *Body Scan*

Now close your eyes, leave all your worries at the door. Allow yourself to relax into the moment. There is only right here, right now.

Clinging to nothing, just be at rest with what is.
(pause)

Focus on your breathing and the words you hear and if your mind gets distracted, let my voice bring you back and then focus again on your breathing.

---

[5] [1] Alcoholics Anonymous Big Book (4th ed.). (2002). Alcoholics Anonymous World Services (Page 59)

Relax now and just breathe.
(pause)

Observe the natural rhythm and flow of your breath.

Take a few moments now, to pay closer attention to it, giving thanks for its presence.
(pause)

Notice the pause at the top of your inhale and again at the bottom of your exhale.
(pause)

Go within, don't think, just breathe.
(pause)

Take a long slow deep breath in and hold it for a moment. Then slowly exhale with a sigh. Allow any tension to melt away.
(pause)

Feel the coolness of the air on the tip of your nose as you inhale and the warmth of the breath as you exhale.
(pause)

Feel the rise of your chest and abdomen on each inhale and the fall on every exhale. As you exhale, let go of any stress or tension, see it floating away, as you gradually relax more deeply with each breath.
(pause)

Grounding ourselves helps us to shed any feelings of anxiety, restlessness, or fear that may be lingering in body or mind.

So, take a few minutes now to feel grounded and simply connected to the earth. Notice the breath as it nourishes every cell of your body.
(pause)

Focused breathing allows your mind to slow down. On your own really focus on your next three breathes as you gently inhale and exhale.
(pause)

Feel the energy that comes from the earth, its strength and stability. Let this energy ground you. Feel that energy come through the souls of your feet, like a breeze flowing through and over your entire body.
(pause)

Now, feeling that grounded energy, begin to feel a tingle in the tips of your toes and the souls of your feet, know that you are safe, stable, supported and loved.
(pause)

Now, gently bring your focus to your ankles, your calves, your thighs, feeling those muscles relax, as you feel yourself sinking into the surface you are resting upon.
(pause)

Breathe in and breathe out.

Move your focus to your buttocks… and hips, release any tension you may be feeling and allow yourself to drift into a state of deep relaxation.
(pause)

Focus on the base of your spine, relaxing the muscles in your lower back, feel a warmth and think of the strong color red, as this area represents stability, safety, and security.
(pause)

Now allow that feeling of warmth and relaxation to move to your lower abdominal muscles, just below your belly button, and think of the warm color orange, as this area represents creativity and sexual energies.
(pause)

Feel your body relaxing with each breath you take.
(pause)

Move your focus to your upper abdominal muscles, just above your belly button, relax those muscles and feel a warmth and relaxation as you think of the vibrant color yellow, as this area represents will-power, self-esteem, pleasure, and personal responsibility.
(pause)

Breathe in God's love and peace and breathe out all resistance.
(pause)

Now feel the warmth and relaxation move slowly and gently to your heart center, in the middle of your chest and about two inches in, and think of a beautiful color of green, as this area represents self-love, our love for others and governs our relationships.

(pause)

Feel yourself becoming deeper and deeper relaxed, your breath will assist you.

(pause)

Feel the muscles in your upper back and chest release and open. Relax your neck and shoulders and allow the relaxation to flow through your arms, and hands.

Begin to feel a tingle in your fingertips and allow any remaining tension in your body to flow out through your fingertips and be released into nothingness.

(pause)

Slowly move your focus to your throat, feeling the muscles of your throat loosen and open, as you think of the soft color of light blue, as this area represents the ability to speak clearly and effectively.

Unclench your teeth, release your jaw muscles, relax the muscles in your cheeks, and just breathe.

(pause)

Let your focus move to your eyes. Now, relax your eye lids and your eye sockets.

(pause)

Gently, move your focus to the spot near the middle of your forehead, between your eyebrows. Relax your eyebrows and all the muscles in your forehead, and think of the color indigo blue, as this area represents foresight, intuition, clarity, and is driven by openness and imagination.
(pause)

Bring your focus to the very top of your head, the crown of your head, feel a tingle there as you relax the muscles in your scalp, and feel it opening as you think of the majestic color of purple, as this area represents Divine connection, and a higher state of consciousness.
(pause)

Now, imagine a bright and beautiful ribbon of crystalline white light coming from above and tethering you to the heavens. Let that light flow to you and through you, enveloping you in a bubble of love and protection.
(pause)

Take a deep breath in and as you exhale allow any remaining tension to be released from your body. Repeating these words in your mind, "peace begins within, peace begins within."
(pause)

Just breathe and go within.
(pause)

• *Guided Meditation*

Nothing changes if nothing changes. If you want to change, you are going to have to make some decisions. It is not about wishing, dreaming, or wanting to change. Step Three requires making a decision. You must choose to let go and let God direct your thoughts and actions. This is a decision you get to do daily. Remember, we do this one day at a time.

(pause)

As you continue to relax and clear your mind, imagine you are walking in a beautiful park, you see birds in the trees singing, squirrels rushing around on the ground, and you can feel the warmth of the sun on your skin. There are families out strolling with their children and others walking their dogs.

(pause)

You see a couple of benches just ahead of you near the playground where children are running, climbing, and having a wonderful day. As you sit down on the bench you hear two children arguing over a toy. It makes you reflect upon your own life, struggles with those around you, wanting to have your way, perhaps fighting to get what you want from others, and the negative feelings those memories bring wash over you. Those thoughts and feelings exhaust you. Thinking of what trying to force your will has brought you and realizing that it is not working

27

out very well. You reflect on where your best intentions have gotten you.

(pause)

Sure, there are moments where things work out well, however, you know your life is a mess and out of control. You know you are at a crossroads, and you have a choice to keep doing the same things and getting the same results or make a decision to give the God of Your Understanding control over your will and your life. You must decide, God either is or he is not.

(pause)

Breathe in peace and exhale all resistance.

(pause)

When you allow your will to conform with God's will, that is when you use it rightly. Have you ever been told to listen to your gut? If you get still and pause for a moment, it is then that you can begin to listen and feel God gently nudging you toward your next right step. There, inside you is where the change begins. When you listen and begin to know God's will and begin to follow it, you will be amazed.

(pause)

There as you sit on the park bench reflecting, you decide to turn your will and your life over to the care of God, in whatever form you understand God. Take a deep breath and exhale with a sigh. Just be, just go within and feel the comfort, safety, and ease that this brings you.

(pause)

Before you get up and continue your stroll through the park, you pause and say this prayer inside your mind.

"God, I offer myself to thee, to build with me and to do with me as Thou Wilt. Relieve me of the bondage of self, that I may better do Your will. Take away my difficulties, that victory over them, may bear witness, to those I would help, of Thy Power, Thy Love and Thy way of life. May I do your will always."[6]
(pause)

Take a slow breath in and out.
(pause)

As you get up from the bench and continue your walk in the park, you see a couple walking past you, they are pushing a baby stroller. You glance down as they pass and see their baby sleeping peacefully, without a care in the world and you feel that sense of peace and serenity within you. You carry that feeling with you as you make your way to the park exit and continue with the rest of your day.
(pause)

Again, focus on your breathing. Feeling your lungs expand on each inhale and relax on each exhale.
(pause)

Don't think, just breathe.
(pause)

---

[6] [1]Alcoholics Anonymous Big Book (4th ed.). (2002). Alcoholics Anonymous World Services (Page 63)

You may be feeling rejuvenated and have a new feeling of confidence about you. There is more work to be done and you are heading in the right direction, putting one foot in front of the other as you take the third step towards a new freedom and a new happiness.

You know you are ready to take the next right step. **(pause)**

- *Closing*

Start to deepen your breath now and become more aware of your physical body. Take a deep breath in and release it with a sigh. Start to wiggle your fingers and toes, stretch your arms and legs, open your eyes, and come back to the present time and space.

NAMASTE'

Meditation for Step Four

*Step Four: "Made a searching and fearless
moral inventory of ourselves"*[7]

"Surrender is the key to ascending and truly transforming
your life. Surrender in each moment as it comes, and you
will live a life full of rich moments." (Author Unknown)

*This meditation starts with a body scan that assists in relaxation
and focus and leads into the portion specific on Step Four.*

• *Body Scan*

Now close your eyes, leave all your worries at the door.
Allow yourself to relax into the moment. There is only
right here, right now.

Clinging to nothing, just be at rest with what is.
(pause)

Focus on your breathing and the words you hear and if
your mind gets distracted, let my voice bring you back and
then focus again on your breathing.

---

[7] Alcoholics Anonymous Big Book (4th ed.). (2002). Alcoholics Anonymous World
Services. (Page 59)

Relax now and just breathe.
(pause)

Observe the natural rhythm and flow of your breath.

Take a few moments now, to pay closer attention to it, giving thanks for its presence.
(pause)

Notice the pause at the top of your inhale and again at the bottom of your exhale.
(pause)

Go within, don't think, just breathe.
(pause)

Take a long slow deep breath in and hold it for a moment. Then slowly exhale with a sigh. Allow any tension to melt away.
(pause)

Feel the coolness of the air on the tip of your nose as you inhale and the warmth of the breath as you exhale.
(pause)

Feel the rise of your chest and abdomen on each inhale and the fall on every exhale. As you exhale, let go of any stress or tension, see it floating away, as you gradually relax more deeply with each breath.
(pause)

Grounding ourselves helps us to shed any feelings of anxiety, restlessness, or fear that may be lingering in body or mind.

So, take a few minutes now to feel grounded and simply connected to the earth. Notice the breath as it nourishes every cell of your body.
(pause)

Focused breathing allows your mind to slow down. On your own really focus on your next three breathes as you gently inhale and exhale.
(pause)

Feel the energy that comes from the earth, its strength and stability. Let this energy ground you. Feel that energy come through the souls of your feet, like a breeze flowing through and over your entire body.
(pause)

Now, feeling that grounded energy, begin to feel a tingle in the tips of your toes and the souls of your feet, know that you are safe, stable, supported and loved.
(pause)

Now, gently bring your focus to your ankles, your calves, your thighs, feeling those muscles relax, as you feel yourself sinking into the surface you are resting upon.
(pause)

Breathe in and breathe out.

Move your focus to your buttocks… and hips, release any tension you may be feeling and allow yourself to drift into a state of deep relaxation.
(pause)

Focus on the base of your spine, relaxing the muscles in your lower back, feel a warmth and think of the strong color red, as this area represents stability, safety, and security.
(pause)

Now allow that feeling of warmth and relaxation to move to your lower abdominal muscles, just below your belly button, and think of the warm color orange, as this area represents creativity and sexual energies.
(pause)

Feel your body relaxing with each breath you take.
(pause)

Move your focus to your upper abdominal muscles, just above your belly button, relax those muscles and feel a warmth and relaxation as you think of the vibrant color yellow, as this area represents will-power, self-esteem, pleasure, and personal responsibility.
(pause)

Breathe in God's love and peace and breathe out all resistance.
(pause)

Now feel the warmth and relaxation move slowly and gently to your heart center, in the middle of your chest

and about two inches in, and think of a beautiful color of green, as this area represents self-love, our love for others and governs our relationships.

(pause)

Feel yourself becoming deeper and deeper relaxed, your breath will assist you.

(pause)

Feel the muscles in your upper back and chest release and open. Relax your neck and shoulders and allow the relaxation to flow through your arms, and hands.

Begin to feel a tingle in your fingertips and allow any remaining tension in your body to flow out through your fingertips and be released into nothingness.

(pause)

Slowly move your focus to your throat, feeling the muscles of your throat loosen and open, as you think of the soft color of light blue, as this area represents the ability to speak clearly and effectively.

Unclench your teeth, release your jaw muscles, relax the muscles in your cheeks, and just breathe.

(pause)

Let your focus move to your eyes. Now, relax your eye lids and your eye sockets.

(pause)

Gently, move your focus to the spot near the middle of your forehead, between your eyebrows. Relax your eyebrows and all the muscles in your forehead, and think of the color indigo blue, as this area represents foresight, intuition, clarity, and is driven by openness and imagination.
(pause)

Bring your focus to the very top of your head, the crown of your head, feel a tingle there as you relax the muscles in your scalp, and feel it opening as you think of the majestic color of purple, as this area represents Divine connection, and a higher state of consciousness.
(pause)

Now, imagine a bright and beautiful ribbon of crystalline white light coming from above and tethering you to the heavens. Let that light flow to you and through you, enveloping you in a bubble of love and protection.
(pause)

Take a deep breath in and as you exhale allow any remaining tension to be released from your body. Repeating these words in your mind, "peace begins within, peace begins within."
(pause)

Just breathe and go within.
(pause)

• *Guided Meditation*

Step four is a searching and fearless moral inventory of ourselves, not an immoral inventory. We all have assets as well as defects of character. This meditation is about identifying both our strengths and weaknesses and coming to acceptance of these, as well as, having an opportunity for reflection and growth. It is time to get down to the causes and effects of our drinking. Why we drank, used, and tried to control other people, places, and things.
(pause)

There is a lizard that is called a chameleon. The best know quality of a chameleon is its ability to change its color to blend in with its environment. Have you ever thought of yourself as behaving like a chameleon? Trying to change your behavior to fit in with the group you are with? Perhaps, like being an actor in a play, you act accordingly to blend into a group. You do not want others to know who you are, what you are thinking, or how you are really feeling, so you play the part. Changing your behavior is easier than letting others know who you really are, your true self? Sometimes, you may honestly not know who you really are yourself, what you like, what you dislike, or any other quality.
(pause)

It is time to be honest and reflect on who you really are and how you really feel about many aspects of your life. You have already admitted you are powerless over alcohol and that your life has become unmanageable, that you have come to believe a Power greater than yourself could restore you to sanity and to turn your thoughts and actions over to the care to God, as you understand him. Now is the moment to have the courage to take the next step. Your Higher Power is with you and peace begins within.

(pause)

Courage is the principle of Step four. Look into your heart and search your soul. No one else is around, you are safe. What emotions dominate your life? Perhaps fear, shame, guilt, or maybe, regret, failure, self-pity, or self-pride?

(pause)

Now, visualize yourself in a safe quite place. Take a moment, breathe in and exhale slowly with a sigh. Think back to a situation when you were in a dispute or had friction with a friend or loved one. Be an observer of this event, just remember it as if you were remembering a scene in a movie.

(pause)

Who was there? What was happening? Do you remember how you felt, the words that were said or any physical behaviors?

(pause)

Open your heart center and consider this. Have you ever thought of how the other person or people felt?

Do that now, remembering, you are just observing this event. Ask God to help you to recall this situation from a different perspective. See it with your heart.

Just breathe, go within, you are safe.
(pause)

This is how you begin to write an inventory. You just need to get the ball rolling. One person at a time, one situation at a time, however, you must be willing to see both sides of the event. Most of the time we are clear on what the other person did, now we need to be honest with ourselves and see our part in it. Listen with your heart. The truth can set you free, then peace begins within.
(pause)

Breathe in and breathe out.
(pause)

Sometimes we forget to remember the moments when we were the only one in the scenario. Have you ever been mad at yourself? This is the time to get it out, written in black and white. Get it out of your head and on to paper, so it can stop doing laps up there in your mind.
(pause)

There is not a single person on this earth who has not done and said things or been in situation that were bad. You are not alone; you are not a bad person. You are a sick person trying to get well. Your Higher Power is walking this journey with you.
(pause)

These steps are simple, but no one said it was easy. Trust in your Higher Power to guide you. Let go of the word "blame". We are all flawed and doing the best we can with what we know how to do. Remember that you have assets and list them in your inventory. Let peace and serenity into your heart.

(pause)

"Once we have a complete willingness to take inventory, and exert ourselves to do the job thoroughly, a wonderful light falls upon this foggy scene. As we persist, a brand–new kind of confidence is born, and the sense of relief at finally facing ourselves is indescribable. These are the first fruits of Step Four."[8]

Take a deep breathe in and exhale slowly.

(pause)

"If we are painstaking about this phase of our development, we will be amazed before we are halfway through. We are going to know a new freedom and a new happiness. We will not regret the past nor wish to shut the door on it. We will comprehend the word serenity and we will know peace."[9]

(pause)

Now savor the feelings of acceptance and growth, allowing them to fill you with sense of confidence and self-assurance.

You can make positive changes…One day at a time.

---

[8] Alcoholics Anonymous World Services, Inc. (1989). *Twelve steps and Twelve Traditions.* Alcoholics Anonymous World Services. (Pages 49-50)
[9] Alcoholics Anonymous Big Book (4th ed.). (2002). Alcoholics Anonymous World Services (Page 83)

Say to yourself, "With the help of my Higher Power and the steps, I can grow."
(pause)

Progress, not perfection. One Moment at a time, One Step at a time, One Day at a time.
(pause)

• *Closing*

Start to deepen your breath now and become more aware of your physical body. Take a deep breath in and release it with a sigh. Start to wiggle your fingers and toes, stretch your arms and legs, open your eyes, and come back to the present time and space.

NAMASTE'

Meditation for Step Five

Step Five: "Admitted to God, to ourselves, and to another human being the exact nature of our wrongs."[10]

"Surrender is the key to ascending and truly transforming your life. Surrender in each moment as it comes, and you will live a life full of rich moments." (Author Unknown)

This meditation starts with a body scan that assists in relaxation and focus and leads into the portion specific on Step Five.

• **Body Scan**

Now close your eyes, leave all your worries at the door. Allow yourself to relax into the moment. There is only right here, right now.

Clinging to nothing, just be at rest with what is. **(pause)**

Focus on your breathing and the words you hear and if your mind gets distracted, let my voice bring you back and then focus again on your breathing.

---

[10] Alcoholics Anonymous Big Book (4th ed.). (2002). Alcoholics Anonymous World Services. (Page 59)

Relax now and just breathe.

(pause)

Observe the natural rhythm and flow of your breath.

Take a few moments now, to pay closer attention to it, giving thanks for its presence.

(pause)

Notice the pause at the top of your inhale and again at the bottom of your exhale.

(pause)

Go within, don't think, just breathe.

(pause)

Take a long slow deep breath in and hold it for a moment. Then slowly exhale with a sigh. Allow any tension to melt away.

(pause)

Feel the coolness of the air on the tip of your nose as you inhale and the warmth of the breath as you exhale.

(pause)

Feel the rise of your chest and abdomen on each inhale and the fall on every exhale. As you exhale, let go of any stress or tension, see it floating away, as you gradually relax more deeply with each breath.

(pause)

Grounding ourselves helps us to shed any feelings of anxiety, restlessness, or fear that may be lingering in body or mind.

So, take a few minutes now to feel grounded and simply connected to the earth. Notice the breath as it nourishes every cell of your body.
(pause)

Focused breathing allows your mind to slow down. On your own really focus on your next three breathes as you gently inhale and exhale.
(pause)

Feel the energy that comes from the earth, its strength and stability. Let this energy ground you. Feel that energy come through the souls of your feet, like a breeze flowing through and over your entire body.
(pause)

Now, feeling that grounded energy, begin to feel a tingle in the tips of your toes and the souls of your feet, know that you are safe, stable, supported and loved.
(pause)

Now, gently bring your focus to your ankles, your calves, your thighs, feeling those muscles relax, as you feel yourself sinking into the surface you are resting upon.
(pause)

Breathe in and breathe out.

Move your focus to your buttocks... and hips, release any tension you may be feeling and allow yourself to drift into a state of deep relaxation.

(pause)

Focus on the base of your spine, relaxing the muscles in your lower back, feel a warmth and think of the strong color red, as this area represents stability, safety, and security.

(pause)

Now allow that feeling of warmth and relaxation to move to your lower abdominal muscles, just below your belly button, and think of the warm color orange, as this area represents creativity and sexual energies.

(pause)

Feel your body relaxing with each breath you take.

(pause)

Move your focus to your upper abdominal muscles, just above your belly button, relax those muscles and feel a warmth and relaxation as you think of the vibrant color yellow, as this area represents will-power, self-esteem, pleasure, and personal responsibility.

(pause)

Breathe in God's love and peace and breathe out all resistance.

(pause)

Now feel the warmth and relaxation move slowly and gently to your heart center, in the middle of your chest and about two inches in, and think of a beautiful color of green, as this area represents self-love, our love for others and governs our relationships.

(pause)

Feel yourself becoming deeper and deeper relaxed, your breath will assist you.

(pause)

Feel the muscles in your upper back and chest release and open. Relax your neck and shoulders and allow the relaxation to flow through your arms, and hands.

Begin to feel a tingle in your fingertips and allow any remaining tension in your body to flow out through your fingertips and be released into nothingness.

(pause)

Slowly move your focus to your throat, feeling the muscles of your throat loosen and open, as you think of the soft color of light blue, as this area represents the ability to speak clearly and effectively.

Unclench your teeth, release your jaw muscles, relax the muscles in your cheeks, and just breathe.

(pause)

Let your focus move to your eyes. Now, relax your eye lids and your eye sockets.

(pause)

Gently, move your focus to the spot near the middle of your forehead, between your eyebrows. Relax your eyebrows and all the muscles in your forehead, and think of the color indigo blue, as this area represents foresight, intuition, clarity, and is driven by openness and imagination.

(pause)

Bring your focus to the very top of your head, the crown of your head, feel a tingle there as you relax the muscles in your scalp, and feel it opening as you think of the majestic color of purple, as this area represents Divine connection, and a higher state of consciousness.

(pause)

Now, imagine a bright and beautiful ribbon of crystalline white light coming from above and tethering you to the heavens. Let that light flow to you and through you, enveloping you in a bubble of love and protection.

(pause)

Take a deep breath in and as you exhale allow any remaining tension to be released from your body. Repeating these words in your mind, "peace begins within, peace begins within."

(pause)

• *Guided Meditation*

In Step 5, we "admit to God, to ourselves, and to another human being the exact nature of our wrongs."[11] You have chosen a trusted friend to share the work you have done in Step 4, and you are ready to continue your walk on the path to recovery.
(pause)

Use your imagination to see a well-used path that leads to a forest of beautiful tall redwood trees. You have come here with a trusted friend, carrying a heavy backpack with all the work from your 4th step inside. The two of you hike, and talk, and gaze at this breathtaking forest that only the Maker of the Universe could have created. These trees are magnificent and majestic. It is the early morning and no one else is the forest. You can hear birds singing and see light filtering through the treetops. You find yourself in awe of the size of the trees and can only guess how old they must be. As you both continue to walk you come upon a tree that has a wide opening in the trunk and appears to have a cave like shelter. Walking up to look inside you imagine that many others must have come inside to seek shelter from a storm or to a rest a while before they continued their journey. You feel safe and protected from the outside world. You ponder the conversations others may have shared in this place. Although the tree has heard the stories, it shares them with no one.
(pause)

---

[11] Alcoholics Anonymous Big Book (4th ed.). (2002). Alcoholics Anonymous World Services. (Page 59)

You set down your backpacks and find a comfortable place to sit. You have chosen, here, in this special place, is where you will confide in your trusted friend, and share all the work you have done on your fourth step. You have been as thorough as you know how to be in your preparation and here, in this cave like shelter you feel safe. You can feel the presence of your Higher Power and have invited Him to join you and your trusted friend in this conversation.
(pause)

You both sit down and get comfortable. You get your step work out of your backpack and begin to share your story. Slowly, going through each page, you discuss what you have written.
(pause)

Once you get past the first few things, you realize that you are feeling more at ease and come to realize that this is not going to be as bad as you imagined. You find that your friend has experienced many of the same type of situations that you are sharing and shares details of their own experience.
(pause)

As you continue sharing, page by page, you begin to feel as though some of the load you have been carrying has been lifted from you.
(pause)

You are able to breathe a little easier.
(pause)

Your friend may ask if there is anything else that you may have left out or forgotten, that you need to share now. It is vital that you have shared to the best of your ability, leaving nothing out. Secrets keep us sick and keep us from finding the Sunlight of the Spirit. So, you dig deep, and share that one thing, you had thought, you would never tell anyone.

(pause)

Now, having been completely honest and having left nothing out, you experience a new freedom and a new happiness. In time, more may be revealed, and you want or need to do another 4th step on those things that come up in the future. For now, you are beginning to understand that to surrender is to win and those things that weighted you down, no longer have power over you.

(pause)

As you begin to rise to put your backpack on, you notice that it feels much lighter than before. You smile as you realize that the great load that you had carried for so long, has lessened and you are coming to understand the benefits of the 4th and 5th steps.

(pause)

As you continue your hike through the woods, the trees look at bit greener and the sky looks a bit bluer than before. As though you are looking through a new pair of glasses. Upon your way back home, you see a rainbow and it reminds you that the promises are coming true. You smile, knowing your Higher Power is with you.

(pause)

Having completed your 5th step, you take a deep breath and exhale as you relax and move forward on the road of Happy Destiny.

(pause)

• *Closing*

Start to deepen your breath now and become more aware of your physical body. Take a deep breath in and release it with a sigh. Start to wiggle your fingers and toes, stretch your arms and legs, open your eyes, and come back to the present time and space.

NAMASTE'

Meditation for Step Six

Step Six: "Were entirely ready to have God remove all these defects of character."[12]

"Surrender is the key to ascending and truly transforming your life. Surrender in each moment as it comes, and you will live a life full of rich moments." (Author Unknown)

This meditation starts with a body scan that assists in relaxation and focus and leads into the portion specific on Step Six.

• *Body Scan*

Now close your eyes, leave all your worries at the door. Allow yourself to relax into the moment. There is only right here, right now.

Clinging to nothing, just be at rest with what is.
(pause)

Focus on your breathing and the words you hear and if your mind gets distracted, let my voice bring you back and then focus again on your breathing.

---

[12] Alcoholics Anonymous Big Book (4th ed.). (2002). Alcoholics Anonymous World Services. (Page 59)

Relax now and just breathe.
(pause)

Observe the natural rhythm and flow of your breath.

Take a few moments now, to pay closer attention to it, giving thanks for its presence.
(pause)

Notice the pause at the top of your inhale and again at the bottom of your exhale.
(pause)

Go within, don't think, just breathe.
(pause)

Take a long slow deep breath in and hold it for a moment. Then slowly exhale with a sigh. Allow any tension to melt away.
(pause)

Feel the coolness of the air on the tip of your nose as you inhale and the warmth of the breath as you exhale.
(pause)

Feel the rise of your chest and abdomen on each inhale and the fall on every exhale. As you exhale, let go of any stress or tension, see it floating away, as you gradually relax more deeply with each breath.
(pause)

Grounding ourselves helps us to shed any feelings of anxiety, restlessness, or fear that may be lingering in body or mind.

So, take a few minutes now to feel grounded and simply connected to the earth. Notice the breath as it nourishes every cell of your body.
(pause)

Focused breathing allows your mind to slow down. On your own really focus on your next three breathes as you gently inhale and exhale.
(pause)

Feel the energy that comes from the earth, its strength and stability. Let this energy ground you. Feel that energy come through the souls of your feet, like a breeze flowing through and over your entire body.
(pause)

Now, feeling that grounded energy, begin to feel a tingle in the tips of your toes and the souls of your feet, know that you are safe, stable, supported and loved.
(pause)

Now, gently bring your focus to your ankles, your calves, your thighs, feeling those muscles relax, as you feel yourself sinking into the surface you are resting upon.
(pause)

Breathe in and breathe out.

Move your focus to your buttocks… and hips, release any tension you may be feeling and allow yourself to drift into a state of deep relaxation.

(pause)

Focus on the base of your spine, relaxing the muscles in your lower back, feel a warmth and think of the strong color red, as this area represents stability, safety, and security.

(pause)

Now allow that feeling of warmth and relaxation to move to your lower abdominal muscles, just below your belly button, and think of the warm color orange, as this area represents creativity and sexual energies.

(pause)

Feel your body relaxing with each breath you take.

(pause)

Move your focus to your upper abdominal muscles, just above your belly button, relax those muscles and feel a warmth and relaxation as you think of the vibrant color yellow, as this area represents will-power, self-esteem, pleasure, and personal responsibility.

(pause)

Breathe in God's love and peace and breathe out all resistance.

(pause)

Now feel the warmth and relaxation move slowly and gently to your heart center, in the middle of your chest and about two inches in, and think of a beautiful color of green, as this area represents self-love, our love for others and governs our relationships.

(pause)

Feel yourself becoming deeper and deeper relaxed, your breath will assist you.

(pause)

Feel the muscles in your upper back and chest release and open. Relax your neck and shoulders and allow the relaxation to flow through your arms, and hands.

Begin to feel a tingle in your fingertips and allow any remaining tension in your body to flow out through your fingertips and be released into nothingness.

(pause)

Slowly move your focus to your throat, feeling the muscles of your throat loosen and open, as you think of the soft color of light blue, as this area represents the ability to speak clearly and effectively.

Unclench your teeth, release your jaw muscles, relax the muscles in your cheeks, and just breathe.

(pause)

Let your focus move to your eyes. Now, relax your eye lids and your eye sockets.
(pause)

Gently, move your focus to the spot near the middle of your forehead, between your eyebrows. Relax your eyebrows and all the muscles in your forehead, and think of the color indigo blue, as this area represents foresight, intuition, clarity, and is driven by openness and imagination.
(pause)

Bring your focus to the very top of your head, the crown of your head, feel a tingle there as you relax the muscles in your scalp, and feel it opening as you think of the majestic color of purple, as this area represents Divine connection, and a higher state of consciousness.
(pause)

Now, imagine a bright and beautiful ribbon of crystalline white light coming from above and tethering you to the heavens. Let that light flow to you and through you, enveloping you in a bubble of love and protection.
(pause)

Take a deep breath in and as you exhale allow any remaining tension to be released from your body. Repeating these words in your mind, "peace begins within, peace begins within."
(pause)

• *Guided Meditation*

In Step Five, we shared our inventory of ourselves and our life. We learned more about ourselves and our own personal character defects.

Sometimes it is difficult to recognize or admit our own character defects. We look good on the outside but what is really going on inside of us? This is the time you double down on your 3rd Step; "Made a decision to turn our will and our lives over to the care of God as we understood Him."[13]

(pause)

Take a moment now to imagine an entrance into a beautifully landscaped and manicured community. There are flowerbeds overflowing with seasonal flowers of all shapes and color. The hedges are trimmed, and the trees make a lovely canopy above. This is the neighborhood you call home. It is a pleasant drive passed the entrance and you take the winding road to your home. All the lawns are well kept with luscious green grass, mature trees, and dazzling flowerbeds.

You take the turn into your driveway and beam with pride as you see the sign in front of your home that says, "Yard of the Month."

(pause)

---

[13] Alcoholics Anonymous Big Book (4th ed.). (2002). Alcoholics Anonymous World Services. (Page 59)

After parking your car in the garage, you enter your home. The inside of your home does not reflect the well-kept, maintained, and orderly yard that others observe and admire. You look around and decide it is time and you are ready to make some changes on the inside.

You admit that you need to do some housecleaning. You desire to let go of the things that no longer serve you.
(pause)

Your home did not become cluttered over-night. You have spent years hanging onto things that no longer work or are of any service to you. You are accustomed to these things being there, however, you are no longer comfortable and at ease with them in your life. It is time to let go of the outdated, useless things, that you no longer need. You want the inside of your home to resemble the beauty and serenity of the outside.
(pause)

Now is the time for you to do some internal housecleaning and to work on your character flaws, your old habits, old behaviors, and other survival skills that are no longer working for you. Things that you have come to realize are weighing heavy on your heart and mind.
(pause)

Have you identified some of your character defects? Listen to the following list of a few defects and perhaps you will be able to identify some of them within yourself.

Laziness, Pride, Procrastination, Dominance, Lying, Anger, Gossip, Self-pity, Ignoring others, Talking too much, or Impatience.
(pause)

Remember, God only asks that we be willing. No one is perfect. Ask your Higher Power to help you to make progress and to let go of the things to which you cling. Trust in your Higher Power and pray **daily** for guidance and wisdom. Courage and willingness are the key!
(pause)

Now, hear this prayer:

"God, help me become willing to let go of all the things to which I still cling. Help me to be ready and willing to let You remove my defects of character, that Your Will and purpose may take their place in my daily living."[14]
(pause)

Are you ready to make positive changes, if so…

Say to yourself, "through daily prayer and meditation, and with the help of my Higher Power, my sponsor, the fellowship, and the Steps, I can grow."

Remember, progress, not perfection. Life will get better. Sometimes quickly, sometimes slowly.
(pause)

---

[14] Huff, 2007, 12 Step Companion AA Big Book, Version 2.5.9.6., Updated 2020, [Mobile app] Apple/App Store, © 2007 Dean Huff (6th Step Prayer)

The promises tell us that, "We will suddenly realize that God is doing for us what we could not do for ourselves."[15] Are you ready and willing to clean house and allow God to help you make your insides match your outsides? **(pause)**

Feel a smile growing on your face and inside your heart. Now savor the feelings of acceptance and growth, allowing it to fill you with a sense of love, confidence, and self-assurance. **(pause)**

• *Closing*

Start to deepen your breath now and become more aware of your physical body. Take a deep breath in and release it with a sigh. Start to wiggle your fingers and toes, stretch your arms and legs, open your eyes, and come back to the present time and space.

NAMASTE'

---

[15] Alcoholics Anonymous Big Book (4th ed.). (2002). Alcoholics Anonymous World Services (Page 83)

Meditation for Step Seven

Step Seven: "Humbly asked Him to remove our shortcomings."[16]

"Surrender is the key to ascending and truly transforming your life. Surrender in each moment as it comes, and you will live a life full of rich moments." (Author Unknown)

This meditation starts with a body scan that assists in relaxation and focus and leads into the portion specific on Step Seven.

- ***Body Scan***

Now close your eyes, leave all your worries at the door. Allow yourself to relax into the moment. There is only right here, right now.

Clinging to nothing, just be at rest with what is.
(pause)

Focus on your breathing and the words you hear and if your mind gets distracted, let my voice bring you back and then focus again on your breathing.

---

[16] Alcoholics Anonymous Big Book (4th ed.). (2002). Alcoholics Anonymous World Services (Page 59)

Relax now and just breathe.
(pause)

Observe the natural rhythm and flow of your breath.

Take a few moments now, to pay closer attention to it, giving thanks for its presence.
(pause)

Notice the pause at the top of your inhale and again at the bottom of your exhale.
(pause)

Go within, don't think, just breathe.
(pause)

Take a long slow deep breath in and hold it for a moment. Then slowly exhale with a sigh. Allow any tension to melt away.
(pause)

Feel the coolness of the air on the tip of your nose as you inhale and the warmth of the breath as you exhale.
(pause)

Feel the rise of your chest and abdomen on each inhale and the fall on every exhale. As you exhale, let go of any stress or tension, see it floating away, as you gradually relax more deeply with each breath.
(pause)

Grounding ourselves helps us to shed any feelings of anxiety, restlessness, or fear that may be lingering in body or mind.

So, take a few minutes now to feel grounded and simply connected to the earth. Notice the breath as it nourishes every cell of your body.
(pause)

Focused breathing allows your mind to slow down. On your own really focus on your next three breathes as you gently inhale and exhale.
(pause)

Feel the energy that comes from the earth, its strength and stability. Let this energy ground you. Feel that energy come through the souls of your feet, like a breeze flowing through and over your entire body.
(pause)

Now, feeling that grounded energy, begin to feel a tingle in the tips of your toes and the souls of your feet, know that you are safe, stable, supported and loved.
(pause)

Now, gently bring your focus to your ankles, your calves, your thighs, feeling those muscles relax, as you feel yourself sinking into the surface you are resting upon.
(pause)

Breathe in and breathe out.

Move your focus to your buttocks… and hips, release any tension you may be feeling and allow yourself to drift into a state of deep relaxation.

(pause)

Focus on the base of your spine, relaxing the muscles in your lower back, feel a warmth and think of the strong color red, as this area represents stability, safety, and security.

(pause)

Now allow that feeling of warmth and relaxation to move to your lower abdominal muscles, just below your belly button, and think of the warm color orange, as this area represents creativity and sexual energies.

(pause)

Feel your body relaxing with each breath you take.

(pause)

Move your focus to your upper abdominal muscles, just above your belly button, relax those muscles and feel a warmth and relaxation as you think of the vibrant color yellow, as this area represents will-power, self-esteem, pleasure, and personal responsibility.

(pause)

Breathe in God's love and peace and breathe out all resistance.

(pause)

Now feel the warmth and relaxation move slowly and gently to your heart center, in the middle of your chest and about two inches in, and think of a beautiful color of green, as this area represents self-love, our love for others and governs our relationships.
(pause)

Feel yourself becoming deeper and deeper relaxed, your breath will assist you.
(pause)

Feel the muscles in your upper back and chest release and open. Relax your neck and shoulders and allow the relaxation to flow through your arms, and hands.

Begin to feel a tingle in your fingertips and allow any remaining tension in your body to flow out through your fingertips and be released into nothingness.
(pause)

Slowly move your focus to your throat, feeling the muscles of your throat loosen and open, as you think of the soft color of light blue, as this area represents the ability to speak clearly and effectively.

Unclench your teeth, release your jaw muscles, relax the muscles in your cheeks, and just breathe.
(pause)

Let your focus move to your eyes. Now, relax your eye lids and your eye sockets.
(pause)

Gently, move your focus to the spot near the middle of your forehead, between your eyebrows. Relax your eyebrows and all the muscles in your forehead, and think of the color indigo blue, as this area represents foresight, intuition, clarity, and is driven by openness and imagination.
(pause)

Bring your focus to the very top of your head, the crown of your head, feel a tingle there as you relax the muscles in your scalp, and feel it opening as you think of the majestic color of purple, as this area represents Divine connection, and a higher state of consciousness.
(pause)

Now, imagine a bright and beautiful ribbon of crystalline white light coming from above and tethering you to the heavens. Let that light flow to you and through you, enveloping you in a bubble of love and protection.
(pause)

Take a deep breath in and as you exhale allow any remaining tension to be released from your body. Repeating these words in your mind, "peace begins within, peace begins within."
(pause)

• *Guided Meditation*

In Step Six, we "were entirely ready and willing to have God remove all these defects of character."[17] Now on Step Seven, "We *humbly* ask Him to remove our shortcomings"[18], also referred to as defects of character. Humility is the principle behind Step Seven.[19]

(pause)

I want you to relax and daydream, go to the place that you feel most comfortable, and you feel the presence of your Higher Power. It may be in a majestic forest, a mountain top with a 360 degree view of the world around you, maybe a warm beach with soft sand and clear water, or a beautiful cathedral with stained glass and murals, any place that you feel in awe of the wonder and presence of God.

(pause)

In this special place, you know and can feel the presence of a power greater than yourself. You see yourself praying and as you pray you are surrounded, enveloped, by a bright golden crystalline light. It is warm and pleasing and gives you a feeling of peace and safety. In this moment, you feel love and understanding and know you are here for a reason, you are here to ask your Creator for help, and you pray this prayer.

---

[17] Alcoholics Anonymous Big Book (4th ed.). (2002). Alcoholics Anonymous World Services (Page 59)

[18] Alcoholics Anonymous Big Book (4th ed.). (2002). Alcoholics Anonymous World Services (Page 59)

[19] Huff, 2007, 12 Step Companion AA Big Book, Version 2.5.9.6., Updated 2020, [Mobile app] Apple/App Store, © 2007 Dean Huff (Principles)

"My Creator, I am now willing that you should have all of me, good and bad. I pray that you now remove from me every single defect of character which stands in the way of my usefulness to you and my fellows. Grant me strength, as I go out from here, to do your bidding. Amen"[20]
(pause)

After your prayer, you carry this love in your heart. You realize that to surrender is to win. You have the wisdom of the Almighty available to you at any time. In another book, you can read something like this:

A.S.K. – "**Ask** and it will be given to you; **Seek** and you will find; **Knock** and the door will be opened to you."[21] Your Higher Power is ready, willing, and able, you just need to ask. Then you must trust in the Universe to do for you that which you cannot do for yourself.
(pause)

As you rest and listen to your Inner Being, you become aware that this surrender is not a one and done event. It is something you will continue to practice on a daily basis.
(pause)

We are into action and need to allow God to make changes in our character. To do that, we need to know what God's Will is, in correcting a character defect and then to "act

---

[20] Alcoholics Anonymous Big Book (4th ed.). (2002). Alcoholics Anonymous World Services (Page 76)
[21] The Bible. New International Version. Matthew 7:7

as if" we possess that quality. Our actions will change our thinking.

(pause)

You may catch yourself acting out in a character defect and feel a God nudge, reminding you that there is a better way. In that moment of awareness, you are given the opportunity to change. This is the time to use the courage you have asked for in the Serenity Prayer.

(pause)

In the awareness, is the responsibility or opportunity to use your wisdom. The wisdom you have gained while working the steps.

(pause)

Remember, when in doubt, pause and pray for the right word or action. Then, listen with your heart and you will have a simple knowing and recognizing, of what you feel in your soul. That what is right feels good and what is wrong feels bad.

(pause)

Remember, "God could and would if he were sought."[22]

(pause)

These changes in your thoughts and actions will start to replace the survival skills and old ideas that no longer served

---

[22] Alcoholics Anonymous Big Book (4th ed.). (2002). Alcoholics Anonymous World Services (Page 60)

you. As you practice surrender to your Higher Power daily, you will see evidence of positive changes in your life.
(pause)

No one is perfect, and making progress is a wonderful thing that happens one day at a time.
(pause)

• *Closing*

It is time to return from your daydream. Start to deepen your breath now and become more aware of your physical body. Take a deep breath in and release it with a sigh. Start to wiggle your fingers and toes, stretch your arms and legs, open your eyes, and come back to the present time and space.

NAMASTE'

Meditation for Step Eight

Step Eight: "Made a list of all persons we had harmed, and *became willing* to make amends to them all"[23]

"Surrender is the key to ascending and truly transforming your life. Surrender in each moment as it comes, and you will live a life full of rich moments." (Author Unknown)

This meditation starts with a body scan that assists in relaxation and focus and leads into the portion specific on Step Eight.

- ### *Body Scan*

Now close your eyes, leave all your worries at the door. Allow yourself to relax into the moment. There is only right here, right now.

Clinging to nothing, just be at rest with what is.
(pause)

Focus on your breathing and the words you hear and if your mind gets distracted, let my voice bring you back and then focus again on your breathing.

---

[23] Alcoholics Anonymous Big Book (4th ed.). (2002). Alcoholics Anonymous World Services (Page 59)

Relax now and just breathe.
(pause)

Observe the natural rhythm and flow of your breath.

Take a few moments now, to pay closer attention to it, giving thanks for its presence.
(pause)

Notice the pause at the top of your inhale and again at the bottom of your exhale.
(pause)

Go within, don't think, just breathe.
(pause)

Take a long slow deep breath in and hold it for a moment. Then slowly exhale with a sigh. Allow any tension to melt away.
(pause)

Feel the coolness of the air on the tip of your nose as you inhale and the warmth of the breath as you exhale.
(pause)

Feel the rise of your chest and abdomen on each inhale and the fall on every exhale. As you exhale, let go of any stress or tension, see it floating away, as you gradually relax more deeply with each breath.
(pause)

Grounding ourselves helps us to shed any feelings of anxiety, restlessness, or fear that may be lingering in body or mind.

So, take a few minutes now to feel grounded and simply connected to the earth. Notice the breath as it nourishes every cell of your body.
(pause)

Focused breathing allows your mind to slow down. On your own really focus on your next three breathes as you gently inhale and exhale.
(pause)

Feel the energy that comes from the earth, its strength and stability. Let this energy ground you. Feel that energy come through the souls of your feet, like a breeze flowing through and over your entire body.
(pause)

Now, feeling that grounded energy, begin to feel a tingle in the tips of your toes and the souls of your feet, know that you are safe, stable, supported and loved.
(pause)

Now, gently bring your focus to your ankles, your calves, your thighs, feeling those muscles relax, as you feel yourself sinking into the surface you are resting upon.
(pause)

Breathe in and breathe out.

Move your focus to your buttocks… and hips, release any tension you may be feeling and allow yourself to drift into a state of deep relaxation.

(pause)

Focus on the base of your spine, relaxing the muscles in your lower back, feel a warmth and think of the strong color red, as this area represents stability, safety, and security.

(pause)

Now allow that feeling of warmth and relaxation to move to your lower abdominal muscles, just below your belly button, and think of the warm color orange, as this area represents creativity and sexual energies.

(pause)

Feel your body relaxing with each breath you take.

(pause)

Move your focus to your upper abdominal muscles, just above your belly button, relax those muscles and feel a warmth and relaxation as you think of the vibrant color yellow, as this area represents will-power, self-esteem, pleasure, and personal responsibility.

(pause)

Breathe in God's love and peace and breathe out all resistance.

(pause)

Now feel the warmth and relaxation move slowly and gently to your heart center, in the middle of your chest

and about two inches in, and think of a beautiful color of green, as this area represents self-love, our love for others and governs our relationships.

(pause)

Feel yourself becoming deeper and deeper relaxed, your breath will assist you.

(pause)

Feel the muscles in your upper back and chest release and open. Relax your neck and shoulders and allow the relaxation to flow through your arms, and hands.

Begin to feel a tingle in your fingertips and allow any remaining tension in your body to flow out through your fingertips and be released into nothingness.

(pause)

Slowly move your focus to your throat, feeling the muscles of your throat loosen and open, as you think of the soft color of light blue, as this area represents the ability to speak clearly and effectively.

Unclench your teeth, release your jaw muscles, relax the muscles in your cheeks, and just breathe.

(pause)

Let your focus move to your eyes. Now, relax your eye lids and your eye sockets.

(pause)

Gently, move your focus to the spot near the middle of your forehead, between your eyebrows. Relax your eyebrows and all the muscles in your forehead, and think of the color indigo blue, as this area represents foresight, intuition, clarity, and is driven by openness and imagination.

(pause)

Bring your focus to the very top of your head, the crown of your head, feel a tingle there as you relax the muscles in your scalp, and feel it opening as you think of the majestic color of purple, as this area represents Divine connection, and a higher state of consciousness.

(pause)

Now, imagine a bright and beautiful ribbon of crystalline white light coming from above and tethering you to the heavens. Let that light flow to you and through you, enveloping you in a bubble of love and protection.

(pause)

Take a deep breath in and as you exhale allow any remaining tension to be released from your body. Repeating these words in your mind, "peace begins within, peace begins within."

(pause)

• *Guided Meditation*

If you have been honest and thorough from the start, those around you will have seen a change in your words and actions. These changes are subtle in the beginning and hopefully demonstrate a sort of living amends.

In Step 8, we can relax in knowing that *making a list and becoming willing* to make direct amends is all that is asked, and your Higher Power is ready to help you to become willing. You're not working Step 9 yet, it is not time to make your amends, only to become willing.
(pause)

Part of becoming willing, is preparing for making an amends by writing a letter or making note cards. You have prayed and meditated about explaining why you want to make an amends. Perhaps you start your amends by saying.

- My recovery program suggests making an honest effort to make amends for mistakes of the past, or
- That you want to apologize and make amends for hurts you have caused, or maybe
- You hope by taking responsibility for your actions, it may bring healing and forgiveness.

(pause)

Pray for willingness to be honest and humble. Think of the list you have made of those whom you need to make an amends, visualize someone from your list. Prayer and meditation can help you in your choosing.
(pause)

Replay a moment in your mind of when a harm occurred, remember, you are an observer. Just like watching a movie, however, as the observer you can see and feel the emotions of the other person and how your behavior affected them.

Take a moment now and reflect on that.
(pause)

Breathe in and breathe out.
(pause)

This time as you are reviewing a moment in your mind, swap roles with the other person. How would you feel if the roles were reversed?
(pause)

You must not justify, rationalize, or defend the harms you have caused; you must be honest with yourself. You are not here to judge anyone.
(pause)

Listen to the God within you, feel the guidance and love. Pray to your Higher Power to be willing to make your amends, to inspire your thoughts, words, and actions and to know with whom and when to do your amends. Just become willing.
(pause)

Be still, just breathe.
(pause)

• *Closing*

Start to deepen your breath now and become more aware of your physical body. Take a deep breath in and release it with a sigh. Start to wiggle your fingers and toes, stretch your arms and legs, open your eyes, and come back to the present time and space.

NAMASTE'

Meditation for Step Nine

Step Nine: *"Made direct amends to such people wherever possible, except when to do so would injure them or others"*[24]

"Surrender is the key to ascending and truly transforming your life. Surrender in each moment as it comes, and you will live a life full of rich moments." (Author Unknown)

This meditation starts with a body scan that assists in relaxation and focus and leads into the portion specific on Step Nine.

• *Body Scan*

Now close your eyes, leave all your worries at the door. Allow yourself to relax into the moment. There is only right here, right now.

Clinging to nothing, just be at rest with what is.
(pause)

Focus on your breathing and the words you hear and if your mind gets distracted, let my voice bring you back and then focus again on your breathing.

---

[24] Alcoholics Anonymous Big Book (4th ed.). (2002). Alcoholics Anonymous World Services (Page 59)

Relax now and just breathe.
(pause)

Observe the natural rhythm and flow of your breath.

Take a few moments now, to pay closer attention to it, giving thanks for its presence.
(pause)

Notice the pause at the top of your inhale and again at the bottom of your exhale.
(pause)

Go within, don't think, just breathe.
(pause)

Take a long slow deep breath in and hold it for a moment. Then slowly exhale with a sigh. Allow any tension to melt away.
(pause)

Feel the coolness of the air on the tip of your nose as you inhale and the warmth of the breath as you exhale.
(pause)

Feel the rise of your chest and abdomen on each inhale and the fall on every exhale. As you exhale, let go of any stress or tension, see it floating away, as you gradually relax more deeply with each breath.
(pause)

Grounding ourselves helps us to shed any feelings of anxiety, restlessness, or fear that may be lingering in body or mind.

So, take a few minutes now to feel grounded and simply connected to the earth. Notice the breath as it nourishes every cell of your body.

(pause)

Focused breathing allows your mind to slow down. On your own really focus on your next three breathes as you gently inhale and exhale.

(pause)

Feel the energy that comes from the earth, its strength and stability. Let this energy ground you. Feel that energy come through the souls of your feet, like a breeze flowing through and over your entire body.

(pause)

Now, feeling that grounded energy, begin to feel a tingle in the tips of your toes and the souls of your feet, know that you are safe, stable, supported and loved.

(pause)

Now, gently bring your focus to your ankles, your calves, your thighs, feeling those muscles relax, as you feel yourself sinking into the surface you are resting upon.

(pause)

Breathe in and breathe out.

Move your focus to your buttocks… and hips, release any tension you may be feeling and allow yourself to drift into a state of deep relaxation.

(pause)

Focus on the base of your spine, relaxing the muscles in your lower back, feel a warmth and think of the strong color red, as this area represents stability, safety, and security.

(pause)

Now allow that feeling of warmth and relaxation to move to your lower abdominal muscles, just below your belly button, and think of the warm color orange, as this area represents creativity and sexual energies.

(pause)

Feel your body relaxing with each breath you take.

(pause)

Move your focus to your upper abdominal muscles, just above your belly button, relax those muscles and feel a warmth and relaxation as you think of the vibrant color yellow, as this area represents will-power, self-esteem, pleasure, and personal responsibility.

(pause)

Breathe in God's love and peace and breathe out all resistance.

(pause)

Now feel the warmth and relaxation move slowly and gently to your heart center, in the middle of your chest and about two inches in, and think of a beautiful color of green, as this area represents self-love, our love for others and governs our relationships.

(pause)

Feel yourself becoming deeper and deeper relaxed, your breath will assist you.

(pause)

Feel the muscles in your upper back and chest release and open. Relax your neck and shoulders and allow the relaxation to flow through your arms, and hands.

Begin to feel a tingle in your fingertips and allow any remaining tension in your body to flow out through your fingertips and be released into nothingness.

(pause)

Slowly move your focus to your throat, feeling the muscles of your throat loosen and open, as you think of the soft color of light blue, as this area represents the ability to speak clearly and effectively.

Unclench your teeth, release your jaw muscles, relax the muscles in your cheeks, and just breathe.

(pause)

Let your focus move to your eyes. Now, relax your eye lids and your eye sockets.

(pause)

Gently, move your focus to the spot near the middle of your forehead, between your eyebrows. Relax your eyebrows and all the muscles in your forehead, and think of the color indigo blue, as this area represents foresight, intuition, clarity, and is driven by openness and imagination.
(pause)

Bring your focus to the very top of your head, the crown of your head, feel a tingle there as you relax the muscles in your scalp, and feel it opening as you think of the majestic color of purple, as this area represents Divine connection, and a higher state of consciousness.
(pause)

Now, imagine a bright and beautiful ribbon of crystalline white light coming from above and tethering you to the heavens. Let that light flow to you and through you, enveloping you in a bubble of love and protection.
(pause)

Take a deep breath in and as you exhale allow any remaining tension to be released from your body. Repeating these words in your mind, "peace begins within, peace begins within."
(pause)

• *Guided Meditation*

In Step 9, "we make direct amends wherever possible, except when to do so would injure them or others."[25] It is interesting, how many of the people we were resentful toward, are now the ones we need to forgive and ask for forgiveness.

After becoming willing to make your amends, you've spent time in prayer and meditation asking for your Higher Power to direct your thoughts, words, and actions. You have prepared yourself and your amends. Making daily living amends with your changed behavior is a good start. **(pause)**

Going to your list of people you have harmed, choose someone that God has given you willingness to make amends to. With God's help you have released any blame and are prepared to speak calmly and sincerely in making your amends.
(pause)

Hurt people, hurt people. We all start out as innocent babies and growing up changes how we behave and view the world. We all need love, but we don't all get what we need. The person you are making amends to has had tough times just as you have.
(pause)

---

[25] Alcoholics Anonymous Big Book (4th ed.). (2002). Alcoholics Anonymous World Services (Page 59)

Have you ever considered what happened in their life that caused them to act hurtful?
(pause)

Unforgiveness eats at your heart, your peace, and your serenity.

Forgiveness doesn't excuse the behavior or mean the hurt never happened, forgiveness is a choice to not live in the hurt of the past any longer, because that will only continue to hurt you and your soul. Forgiveness is a gift you give to yourself.
(pause)

Take a deep breath in, then exhale all resistance.
(pause)

Take a moment to check in with your body and feel a lightness as you release all the negativity within you that you held towards that person. When you release the burden, it lightens the load you carry.
(pause)

It takes just as much courage, strength and, humility to ask for forgiveness, as it does to give forgiveness.
(pause)

Consider now, someone else you need to make direct amends with.

Pray for your Higher Power to inspire your thoughts, words, and actions and to know the right time to do your amends.

Ask your Higher Power to help you know when to be slow to speak and quick to listen.
(pause)

Visualize yourself calmly explaining that by taking responsibility for your past actions, you hope it might bring healing.

You see yourself recounting your poor behavior and explain that you would like to make amends for your mistakes from the past.
(pause)

After sincerely apologizing for all these things, you ask for forgiveness and ask if there is any harm that you have left out and if you can do anything to make things right.

Then, you sit there and do not say anything else. You allow the other person to speak uninterrupted.
(pause)

Now see yourself being silent and listening to the other person, not interrupting. Honestly focusing on what the other person is saying, while you are silent and without saying another word.
(pause)

Having made your amends, you now have cleaned up your side of the street. You are now free of the burden. Regardless of whether you receive forgiveness or not, you have done the next right thing. Now take a deep breath and let your stress dissolve and feel it melt away.
(pause)

Focus on the peace, love, warmth, and serenity that flows through you as you feel that weight you carried for so long, just disappear.
(pause)

Take another deep breath in and exhale with a big sigh. Know that the God of your understanding, loves you always and forgives you always when you are sincerely trying to do His will. Feel that crystalline white light that came from above and tethers you to the heavens, continue to flow to you and through you, enveloping you in love and acceptance.
(pause)

Be still and know that peace begins within.
(pause)

Take a deep breath in and allow God's love to fill you from within. Don't think, just breathe. Let yourself be filled to overflowing.
(pause)

Your Higher Power loves you and wants you to love yourself and others. God wants you to be happy, joyous, and free.
(pause)

Just breathe, be still and know, all is well.
(pause)

• *Closing*

Start to deepen your breath now and become more aware of your physical body. Take a deep breath in and release it with a sigh. Start to wiggle your fingers and toes, stretch your arms and legs, open your eyes, and come back to the present time and space.

NAMASTE'

Meditation for Step Ten

Step Ten: *"Continued to take personal inventory and when we were wrong promptly admitted it"*[26]

"Surrender is the key to ascending and truly transforming your life. Surrender in each moment as it comes, and you will live a life full of rich moments." (Author Unknown)

This meditation starts with a body scan that assists in relaxation and focus and leads into the portion specific on Step Ten.

• *Body Scan*

Now close your eyes, leave all your worries at the door. Allow yourself to relax into the moment. There is only right here, right now.

Clinging to nothing, just be at rest with what is.
(pause)

Focus on your breathing and the words you hear and if your mind gets distracted, let my voice bring you back and then focus again on your breathing.

---

[26] Alcoholics Anonymous Big Book (4th ed.). (2002). Alcoholics Anonymous World Services (Page 59)

Relax now and just breathe.
(pause)

Observe the natural rhythm and flow of your breath.

Take a few moments now, to pay closer attention to it, giving thanks for its presence.
(pause)

Notice the pause at the top of your inhale and again at the bottom of your exhale.
(pause)

Go within, don't think, just breathe.
(pause)

Take a long slow deep breath in and hold it for a moment. Then slowly exhale with a sigh. Allow any tension to melt away.
(pause)

Feel the coolness of the air on the tip of your nose as you inhale and the warmth of the breath as you exhale.
(pause)

Feel the rise of your chest and abdomen on each inhale and the fall on every exhale. As you exhale, let go of any stress or tension, see it floating away, as you gradually relax more deeply with each breath.
(pause)

Grounding ourselves helps us to shed any feelings of anxiety, restlessness, or fear that may be lingering in body or mind.

So, take a few minutes now to feel grounded and simply connected to the earth. Notice the breath as it nourishes every cell of your body.
(pause)

Focused breathing allows your mind to slow down. On your own really focus on your next three breathes as you gently inhale and exhale.
(pause)

Feel the energy that comes from the earth, its strength and stability. Let this energy ground you. Feel that energy come through the souls of your feet, like a breeze flowing through and over your entire body.
(pause)

Now, feeling that grounded energy, begin to feel a tingle in the tips of your toes and the souls of your feet, know that you are safe, stable, supported and loved.
(pause)

Now, gently bring your focus to your ankles, your calves, your thighs, feeling those muscles relax, as you feel yourself sinking into the surface you are resting upon.
(pause)

Breathe in and breathe out.

Move your focus to your buttocks… and hips, release any tension you may be feeling and allow yourself to drift into a state of deep relaxation.

(pause)

Focus on the base of your spine, relaxing the muscles in your lower back, feel a warmth and think of the strong color red, as this area represents stability, safety, and security.

(pause)

Now allow that feeling of warmth and relaxation to move to your lower abdominal muscles, just below your belly button, and think of the warm color orange, as this area represents creativity and sexual energies.

(pause)

Feel your body relaxing with each breath you take.

(pause)

Move your focus to your upper abdominal muscles, just above your belly button, relax those muscles and feel a warmth and relaxation as you think of the vibrant color yellow, as this area represents will-power, self-esteem, pleasure, and personal responsibility.

(pause)

Breathe in God's love and peace and breathe out all resistance.

(pause)

Now feel the warmth and relaxation move slowly and gently to your heart center, in the middle of your chest and about two inches in, and think of a beautiful color of green, as this area represents self-love, our love for others and governs our relationships.

(pause)

Feel yourself becoming deeper and deeper relaxed, your breath will assist you.

(pause)

Feel the muscles in your upper back and chest release and open. Relax your neck and shoulders and allow the relaxation to flow through your arms, and hands.

Begin to feel a tingle in your fingertips and allow any remaining tension in your body to flow out through your fingertips and be released into nothingness.

(pause)

Slowly move your focus to your throat, feeling the muscles of your throat loosen and open, as you think of the soft color of light blue, as this area represents the ability to speak clearly and effectively.

Unclench your teeth, release your jaw muscles, relax the muscles in your cheeks, and just breathe.

(pause)

Let your focus move to your eyes. Now, relax your eye lids and your eye sockets.

(pause)

Gently, move your focus to the spot near the middle of your forehead, between your eyebrows. Relax your eyebrows and all the muscles in your forehead, and think of the color indigo blue, as this area represents foresight, intuition, clarity, and is driven by openness and imagination.

(pause)

Bring your focus to the very top of your head, the crown of your head, feel a tingle there as you relax the muscles in your scalp, and feel it opening as you think of the majestic color of purple, as this area represents Divine connection, and a higher state of consciousness.

(pause)

Now, imagine a bright and beautiful ribbon of crystalline white light coming from above and tethering you to the heavens. Let that light flow to you and through you, enveloping you in a bubble of love and protection.

(pause)

Take a deep breath in and as you exhale allow any remaining tension to be released from your body. Repeating these words in your mind, "peace begins within, peace begins within."

(pause)

• *Guided Meditation*

Have you ever had an emotional hangover? That unpleasant feeling inside your heart and gut as the direct result of negative emotions and negative behavior. When in doubt, remember to trust your inner being, the God within each of us. What is right feels good and what is wrong feels bad.

Step Ten helps us review situations and actions in our daily life to check if we are practicing what we have learned in the first nine steps. Sometimes, we can do a "spot check" in the moment and recognize whether we have harmed someone by our words or actions and promptly admit it to ourselves and to them. We correct our behavior on the spot and make amends if needed. Sometimes, at the end of the day when we do a mental review of the day, we might recognize where during the day we were out of line and need to make changes or amends. Then there are other instances that are glaring and there is no doubt that we are disturbed and need to do a formal fourth step on this situation or person. **(pause)**

Take a deep breath in and exhale slowly.
(pause)

Honest evaluation is what is needed to avoid emotional hangovers and the loss of serenity.
(pause)

Focus for a moment on your breathing, relax and let your mind reflect to a recent experience that you would have benefitted from using a "spot check."

What does that memory make you feel?
(pause)

Now, play that memory in your mind again and see yourself recognizing your actions, doing a "spot check," honestly seeing your behavior, and then being willing to admit your error, ask for forgiveness and make changes.

How does this feel in your heart?
(pause)

Take a deep breath in and exhale slowly.
(pause)

Now imagine it is the end of this day, and you are taking a moment to pause and review today's affairs.

Think of the things that went well.

Did you reach out to someone today?
(pause)

Were there times you were kind, courteous, or helpful?

Were there times you recognize selfishness, disrespect, or dishonesty?
(pause)

Try to visualize how you may have done better.
(pause)

Ask God to help you learn from this and not repeat injurious behavior.

Ask yourself, do you need to make an amends?

Do you need to give forgiveness?

Do you need to pray for someone that offended you?
(pause)

Take a deep breath in and exhale slowly.
(pause)

Perhaps, there is a situation that has been bothering you for a while. Take the time to do a thoughtful review and look at the situation as the observer. Then praying to the God of your understanding and speaking with another person about that situation would be a good idea. This may be an opportunity for growth and change. You are worth it!
(pause)

Remember, nothing changes if nothing changes.
(pause)

Breathe in and breath out.
(pause)

Step ten is a tool you use daily, and it will assist you in your emotional sobriety.

(pause)

Take another deep breath in and exhale with a big sigh.
(pause)

Be still and know that peace begins within.
(pause)

Take a deep breath in and allow God's love and peace to flow into your soul....... Don't think, just breathe, just feel.
(pause)

The Maker of the Universe loves you and wants you to love yourself and others. God wants you to be happy, joyous, and free.
(pause)

• *Closing*

Start to deepen your breath now and become more aware of your physical body. Take a deep breath in and release it with a sigh. Start to wiggle your fingers and toes, stretch your arms and legs, open your eyes, and come back to the present time and space.

NAMASTE'

Meditation for Step Eleven

Step Eleven: *"Sought through prayer and meditation to improve our conscious contact with God as we understood Him, praying only for knowledge of His will for us and the power to carry that out"*[27]

Surrender is the key to ascending and truly transforming your life. Surrender in each moment as it comes, and you will live a life full of rich moments. (Author Unknown)

This meditation starts with a body scan that assists in relaxation and focus and leads into the portion specific on Step Eleven.

• *Body Scan*

Now close your eyes, leave all your worries at the door. Allow yourself to relax into the moment. There is only right here, right now.

Clinging to nothing, just be at rest with what is.
(pause)

---

[27] Alcoholics Anonymous Big Book (4th ed.). (2002). Alcoholics Anonymous World Services (Page 59)

Focus on your breathing and the words you hear and if your mind gets distracted, let my voice bring you back and then focus again on your breathing.

Relax now and just breathe.
(pause)

Observe the natural rhythm and flow of your breath.

Take a few moments now, to pay closer attention to it, giving thanks for its presence.
(pause)

Notice the pause at the top of your inhale and again at the bottom of your exhale.
(pause)

Go within, don't think, just breathe.
(pause)

Take a long slow deep breath in and hold it for a moment. Then slowly exhale with a sigh. Allow any tension to melt away.
(pause)

Feel the coolness of the air on the tip of your nose as you inhale and the warmth of the breath as you exhale.
(pause)

Feel the rise of your chest and abdomen on each inhale and the fall on every exhale. As you exhale, let go of any stress or tension, see it floating away, as you gradually relax more deeply with each breath.

(pause)

Grounding ourselves helps us to shed any feelings of anxiety, restlessness, or fear that may be lingering in body or mind.

So, take a few minutes now to feel grounded and simply connected to the earth. Notice the breath as it nourishes every cell of your body.

(pause)

Focused breathing allows your mind to slow down. On your own really focus on your next three breathes as you gently inhale and exhale.

(pause)

Feel the energy that comes from the earth, its strength and stability. Let this energy ground you. Feel that energy come through the souls of your feet, like a breeze flowing through and over your entire body.

(pause)

Now, feeling that grounded energy, begin to feel a tingle in the tips of your toes and the souls of your feet, know that you are safe, stable, supported and loved.

(pause)

Now, gently bring your focus to your ankles, your calves, your thighs, feeling those muscles relax, as you feel yourself sinking into the surface you are resting upon.
(pause)

Breathe in and breathe out.

Move your focus to your buttocks… and hips, release any tension you may be feeling and allow yourself to drift into a state of deep relaxation.
(pause)

Focus on the base of your spine, relaxing the muscles in your lower back, feel a warmth and think of the strong color red, as this area represents stability, safety, and security.
(pause)

Now allow that feeling of warmth and relaxation to move to your lower abdominal muscles, just below your belly button, and think of the warm color orange, as this area represents creativity and sexual energies.
(pause)

Feel your body relaxing with each breath you take.
(pause)

Move your focus to your upper abdominal muscles, just above your belly button, relax those muscles and feel a warmth and relaxation as you think of the vibrant color

yellow, as this area represents will-power, self-esteem, pleasure, and personal responsibility.
(pause)

Breathe in God's love and peace and breathe out all resistance.
(pause)

Now feel the warmth and relaxation move slowly and gently to your heart center, in the middle of your chest and about two inches in, and think of a beautiful color of green, as this area represents self-love, our love for others and governs our relationships.
(pause)

Feel yourself becoming deeper and deeper relaxed, your breath will assist you.
(pause)

Feel the muscles in your upper back and chest release and open. Relax your neck and shoulders and allow the relaxation to flow through your arms, and hands.

Begin to feel a tingle in your fingertips and allow any remaining tension in your body to flow out through your fingertips and be released into nothingness.
(pause)

Slowly move your focus to your throat, feeling the muscles of your throat loosen and open, as you think of the soft

color of light blue, as this area represents the ability to speak clearly and effectively.

Unclench your teeth, release your jaw muscles, relax the muscles in your cheeks, and just breathe.
(pause)

Let your focus move to your eyes. Now, relax your eye lids and your eye sockets.
(pause)

Gently, move your focus to the spot near the middle of your forehead, between your eyebrows. Relax your eyebrows and all the muscles in your forehead, and think of the color indigo blue, as this area represents foresight, intuition, clarity, and is driven by openness and imagination.
(pause)

Bring your focus to the very top of your head, the crown of your head, feel a tingle there as you relax the muscles in your scalp, and feel it opening as you think of the majestic color of purple, as this area represents Divine connection, and a higher state of consciousness.
(pause)

Now, imagine a bright and beautiful ribbon of crystalline white light coming from above and tethering you to the heavens. Let that light flow to you and through you, enveloping you in a bubble of love and protection.
(pause)

Take a deep breath in and as you exhale allow any remaining tension to be released from your body. Repeating these words in your mind, "peace begins within, peace begins within."

(pause)

- ### *Guided Meditation*

Relax and hear these words,

"Meditation is something that can always be further developed. It has no boundaries, either of height or width. Aided by such instruction and example as we can find, it is essentially an individual adventure, something each one of us works out in his own way. But its object is always the same; to improve our conscious contact with God, with His grace, wisdom, and love. And let us always remember that meditation is, intensely practical. One of its first fruits is emotional balance. With it we can broaden and deepen the channel between ourselves and God, as we understand him."[28]

(pause)

Your Higher Power has infinite wisdom, and with prayer and meditation, this is how you tune in and tap into that source of love, guidance, and wisdom.

(pause)

---

[28] The 12 Steps and 12 Traditions - Pages 101-102

Your Higher Power loves you and forgives you and wants you to love and forgive yourself and others. God wants you to be happy, joyous, and free.
(pause)

Now surrender your mind, body, spirit, and emotions to the Creator of the Universe.

Feel the presents of unconditional love.

Focus on your heart center and your breath. Breathe in peace and stillness to your heart center.
(pause)

Pray now in this moment, as you go into meditation, to feel God's gentle nudges and to have the courage to trust Him.
(pause)

Connecting to your heart, go deeper and deeper.
Focus on the intention to open your heart to God.
Sink deeper and deeper into relaxation.
(pause)

Your Higher Power connects with you through your feelings.
(pause)

Just Breathe...Feel the steady rhythm of your breath.
(pause)

Feel all your muscles relax and feel the weight of your body pressing into the surface below you, let any tensing in your body just melt away.

(pause)

Release any thoughts weighing heavy upon you.

Be willing and ask your Higher Power to take it and see it float away, feel the lightness in your body and soul.

(pause)

Concentrate on your breathing, the rhythm of your breathing and, tap into what you are feeling in your heart, allowing yourself to feel the connection to the God within you.

(pause)

Release any expectation, fear, or resistance and open yourself up to the feeling of guidance and love from the God of your understanding. Tune into the safe, stable love of your Higher Power.

(pause)

Receive healing, love, support, and nurturing.

Feel gratitude and a lightness as your feel your heart opening more.

(pause)

Relax as you go deeper and deeper into your heart.

God loves you and is always with you and just waiting for you to reach out.

(pause)

You need a willingness to reach out to your Higher Power and ask for help.

Just Breathe....

(pause)

Now feel this beautiful pure light of God's love come into you, into your mind, into your body and into your spirit. Feel the warmth and peace with each breath you take... Just be still and feel this in every cell of your body, this unconditional love of your Higher Power.

(pause)

Be willing to ask and listen to your Higher Power, "What is my next right step and help me to take it."

(pause)

Do you have something weighing heavy on your heart? Is something holding you back? Drop that thing that is pulling you down and give it to God. In this quiet, peaceful, and safe place inside of you, share your concern with your Higher Power and ask your Higher Power for guidance... Be willing to listen and then be still.

(pause)

Just breathe and listen.

(pause)

A word or phrase, perhaps images come into your mind now, these are from your Higher Power. Let yourself receive these and then pause and let them resonate inside you.
(pause)

Again, ask your Higher Power for help in any area of your life that you are struggling with and after you ask God for help, say, "I am willing to listen for your answer" then be still.
(pause)

As you relax and breathe, take note of feelings, words, or images.
(pause)

God has perfect timing and sometimes the answer might be, to do nothing and just wait. Trust God…let go of control.
(pause)

Relax, just breathe.
(pause)

Do you need to ask your Higher Power for help in any of these areas…for serenity, acceptance, for courage or wisdom, maybe to take away a survival skill that no longer serves you, to remember to pause and pray, to give forgiveness, for honesty or humility?

Perhaps you need to ask God to help you to be willing to be willing?
(pause)

Ask the God of your understanding for guidance in any area that you need guidance, have questions or decisions that need to be made. Do you have a behavior pattern you want to let go of? Surrender your questions to the Maker of the Universe and listen with your heart.

(pause)

Feel the messages, guidance, or insight you receive. Feel the love in the guidance you receive and see it with your spiritual eyes.

Know the Maker of the Universe, loves you unconditionally and wants the best for you.

Be still and trust the Source of Infinite Intelligence.

(pause)

Listen to the God within you, feel the guidance and love and ask God to help you perceive His will for you.

(pause)

Ask your Higher Power for a shield of love and protection.

In your mind, say this prayer.

"God, I ask to have your love and protection around me today and always. Guide me and teach me to know your will in my heart and to have the courage to trust you and to do your will."

(pause)

Keep your heart open to receive that wisdom, truth, love, and insight and thank the Maker of the Universe in advance for the blessings that are prepared for you.

Send feelings of love, gratitude and thanks to the God of your understanding.
(pause)

- *Closing*

Start to deepen your breath now and become more aware of your physical body. Take a couple of deep breaths in and out. Stretch your arms and legs, begin to wiggle your fingers and toes, open your eyes, and come back to this space and time.

NAMASTE'

Meditation for Step Twelve

Step Twelve: *"Having had a spiritual awaking as the result of these steps, we tried to carry this message to alcoholics, and to practice these principles in all our affairs."*[29]

Surrender is the key to ascending and truly transforming your life. Surrender in each moment as it comes, and you will live a life full of rich moments. (Author Unknown)

This meditation starts with a body scan that assists in relaxation and focus and leads into the portion specific on Step Twelve.

• *Body Scan*

Now close your eyes, leave all your worries at the door. Allow yourself to relax into the moment. There is only right here, right now.

Clinging to nothing, just be at rest with what is.
(pause)

Focus on your breathing and the words you hear and if your mind gets distracted, let my voice bring you back and then focus again on your breathing.

---

[29] Alcoholics Anonymous Big Book (4th ed.). (2002). Alcoholics Anonymous World Services (Page 60)

Relax now and just breathe.
(pause)

Observe the natural rhythm and flow of your breath.

Take a few moments now, to pay closer attention to it, giving thanks for its presence.
(pause)

Notice the pause at the top of your inhale and again at the bottom of your exhale.
(pause)

Go within, don't think, just breathe.
(pause)

Take a long slow deep breath in and hold it for a moment. Then slowly exhale with a sigh. Allow any tension to melt away.
(pause)

Feel the coolness of the air on the tip of your nose as you inhale and the warmth of the breath as you exhale.
(pause)

Feel the rise of your chest and abdomen on each inhale and the fall on every exhale. As you exhale, let go of any stress or tension, see it floating away, as you gradually relax more deeply with each breath.
(pause)

Grounding ourselves helps us to shed any feelings of anxiety, restlessness, or fear that may be lingering in body or mind.

So, take a few minutes now to feel grounded and simply connected to the earth. Notice the breath as it nourishes every cell of your body.
(pause)

Focused breathing allows your mind to slow down. On your own really focus on your next three breathes as you gently inhale and exhale.
(pause)

Feel the energy that comes from the earth, its strength and stability. Let this energy ground you. Feel that energy come through the souls of your feet, like a breeze flowing through and over your entire body.
(pause)

Now, feeling that grounded energy, begin to feel a tingle in the tips of your toes and the souls of your feet, know that you are safe, stable, supported and loved.
(pause)

Now, gently bring your focus to your ankles, your calves, your thighs, feeling those muscles relax, as you feel yourself sinking into the surface you are resting upon.
(pause)

Breathe in and breathe out.

Move your focus to your buttocks… and hips, release any tension you may be feeling and allow yourself to drift into a state of deep relaxation.

(pause)

Focus on the base of your spine, relaxing the muscles in your lower back, feel a warmth and think of the strong color red, as this area represents stability, safety, and security.

(pause)

Now allow that feeling of warmth and relaxation to move to your lower abdominal muscles, just below your belly button, and think of the warm color orange, as this area represents creativity and sexual energies.

(pause)

Feel your body relaxing with each breath you take.

(pause)

Move your focus to your upper abdominal muscles, just above your belly button, relax those muscles and feel a warmth and relaxation as you think of the vibrant color yellow, as this area represents will-power, self-esteem, pleasure, and personal responsibility.

(pause)

Breathe in God's love and peace and breathe out all resistance.

(pause)

Now feel the warmth and relaxation move slowly and gently to your heart center, in the middle of your chest and about two inches in, and think of a beautiful color of green, as this area represents self-love, our love for others and governs our relationships.

(pause)

Feel yourself becoming deeper and deeper relaxed, your breath will assist you.

(pause)

Feel the muscles in your upper back and chest release and open. Relax your neck and shoulders and allow the relaxation to flow through your arms, and hands.

Begin to feel a tingle in your fingertips and allow any remaining tension in your body to flow out through your fingertips and be released into nothingness.

(pause)

Slowly move your focus to your throat, feeling the muscles of your throat loosen and open, as you think of the soft color of light blue, as this area represents the ability to speak clearly and effectively.

Unclench your teeth, release your jaw muscles, relax the muscles in your cheeks, and just breathe.

(pause)

Let your focus move to your eyes. Now, relax your eye lids and your eye sockets.

(pause)

Gently, move your focus to the spot near the middle of your forehead, between your eyebrows. Relax your eyebrows and all the muscles in your forehead, and think of the color indigo blue, as this area represents foresight, intuition, clarity, and is driven by openness and imagination.

(pause)

Bring your focus to the very top of your head, the crown of your head, feel a tingle there as you relax the muscles in your scalp, and feel it opening as you think of the majestic color of purple, as this area represents Divine connection, and a higher state of consciousness.

(pause)

Now, imagine a bright and beautiful ribbon of crystalline white light coming from above and tethering you to the heavens. Let that light flow to you and through you, enveloping you in a bubble of love and protection.

(pause)

Take a deep breath in and as you exhale allow any remaining tension to be released from your body. Repeating these words in your mind, "peace begins within, peace begins within."

(pause)

• *Guided Meditation*

Step twelve says, that "as a result of taking the previous eleven steps, we will have had a spiritual awakening and we try to carry this message to the alcoholic and to practice these principles in all our affairs."[30]

Just how do we do that?
(pause)

Imagine yourself in a situation where you are aware of someone else that is struggling with alcoholism. See yourself sitting down with that person and sharing with them your experience with alcoholism (what it was like), sharing the strength you received in working the steps, (what happened) and sharing the hope that they too, can also have what you have, (what it's like now).

Visualize this now.
(pause)

Carrying the message does not have to be complicated. Others may see a positive change in your behavior and ask how you were able to stop drinking and stay sober. Being honest, open, and willing, as well as having a relationship with a Power greater than ourselves can help in seeing opportunities to carry the message inside and outside of the rooms of recovery.
(pause)

---

[30] Alcoholics Anonymous Big Book (4th ed.). (2002). Alcoholics Anonymous World Services (Page 60)

There are numerous ways to be of service. Being a sponsor, sharing in a meeting, cleaning up after a meeting, setting up a meeting, making coffee, leading a meeting and this list goes on and on. Reflect now, on how you have been or could be of service to others.
(pause)

What exactly are the principles? We learn them as we take the steps.

Step One is <u>Honesty</u>, Step Two is <u>Hope</u>, Step Three is <u>Faith</u>, Step Four is <u>Courage</u>, Step Five is <u>Integrity</u>, Step Six is <u>Willingness</u>, Step Seven is <u>Humility</u>, Step Eight is <u>Brotherly Love</u>, Step Nine is <u>Justice</u>, Step Ten is <u>Perseverance</u>, Step Eleven is <u>Spirituality</u>, and Step Twelve is <u>Service</u>.[31]
(pause)

As we took the steps, the principles became a part of our everyday life. So, whether we are at home, work, or any other place, these principles become second nature to us. We practice these principles in all our affairs and understand that no one is perfect. We are not saints.
(pause)

If we are willing to grow, we will make progress.
(pause)

---

[31] Huff, 2007, 12 Step Companion AA Big Book, Version 2.5.9.6., Updated 2020, [Mobile app] Apple/App Store, © 2007 Dean Huff (Principles)

You are never alone in your progress. The God of your understanding is with you, and can and will help you, if you seek Him.

(pause)

Breathe in and breathe out.

(pause)

Remember, God nudges you in many ways. Stay open and recognize what you feel in your soul. That what is right feels good and what is wrong feels bad. To live in harmony with your fellow man, say, "yes" to the good and say, "no" to the bad.

(pause)

Keep doing the next right thing, one day at a time, one step at a time, one moment at a time.

(pause)

• *Closing*

Start to deepen your breath now and become more aware of your physical body. Take a deep breath in and release it with a sigh. Start to wiggle your fingers and toes, stretch your arms and legs, open your eyes, and come back to the present time and space.

NAMASTE'

PART TWO

The 12 Principles

Meditation on Recovery Principles for Steps One, Two, Three and Four

What exactly are the principles? We
learn them as we take the steps.
*Step One is <u>Honesty</u>, Step Two is <u>Hope</u>, Step
Three is <u>Faith</u>, Step Four is <u>Courage</u>.*[32]

"Surrender is the key to ascending and truly transforming your life. Surrender in each moment as it comes, and you will live a life full of rich moments." (Author Unknown)

This meditation starts with a body scan that assists in relaxation and focus and leads into the portion specific on AA Principles for Steps One, Two, Three and Four.

• *Body Scan*

Now close your eyes, leave all your worries at the door. Allow yourself to relax into the moment. There is only right here, right now.

Clinging to nothing, just be at rest with what is.
(pause)

---

[32] Huff, 2007, 12 Step Companion AA Big Book, Version 2.5.9.6., Updated 2020, [Mobile app] Apple/App Store, © 2007 Dean Huff (Principles)

Focus on your breathing and the words you hear and if your mind gets distracted, let my voice bring you back and then focus again on your breathing.

Relax now and just breathe.
(pause)

Observe the natural rhythm and flow of your breath.

Take a few moments now, to pay closer attention to it, giving thanks for its presence.
(pause)

Notice the pause at the top of your inhale and again at the bottom of your exhale.
(pause)

Go within, don't think, just breathe.
(pause)

Take a long slow deep breath in and hold it for a moment. Then slowly exhale with a sigh. Allow any tension to melt away.
(pause)

Feel the coolness of the air on the tip of your nose as you inhale and the warmth of the breath as you exhale.
(pause)

Feel the rise of your chest and abdomen on each inhale and the fall on every exhale. As you exhale, let go of any stress or tension, see it floating away, as you gradually relax more deeply with each breath.

(pause)

Grounding ourselves helps us to shed any feelings of anxiety, restlessness, or fear that may be lingering in body or mind.

So, take a few minutes now to feel grounded and simply connected to the earth. Notice the breath as it nourishes every cell of your body.

(pause)

Focused breathing allows your mind to slow down. On your own really focus on your next three breathes as you gently inhale and exhale.

(pause)

Feel the energy that comes from the earth, its strength and stability. Let this energy ground you. Feel that energy come through the souls of your feet, like a breeze flowing through and over your entire body.

(pause)

Now, feeling that grounded energy, begin to feel a tingle in the tips of your toes and the souls of your feet, know that you are safe, stable, supported and loved.

(pause)

Now, gently bring your focus to your ankles, your calves, your thighs, feeling those muscles relax, as you feel yourself sinking into the surface you are resting upon.

(pause)

Breathe in and breathe out.

Move your focus to your buttocks… and hips, release any tension and allow yourself to drift into a state of deep relaxation.
(pause)

Focus on the base of your spine, relaxing the muscles in your lower back, feel a warmth and think of the strong color red, as this area represents stability, safety, and security.
(pause)

Now allow that feeling of warmth and relaxation to move to your lower abdominal muscles, just below your belly button, and think of the warm color orange, as this area represents creativity and sexual energies.
(pause)

Feel your body relaxing with each breath you take.
(pause)

Move your focus to your upper abdominal muscles, just above your belly button, relax those muscles and feel a warmth and relaxation as you think of the vibrant color yellow, as this area represents will-power, self-esteem, pleasure, and personal responsibility.
(pause)

Breathe in God's love and peace and breathe out all resistance.
(pause)

Now feel the warmth and relaxation move slowly and gently to your heart center, in the middle of your chest and about two inches in, and think of a beautiful color of green, as this area represents self-love, our love for others and governs our relationships.
(pause)

Feel yourself becoming deeper and deeper relaxed, your breath will assist you.
(pause)

Feel the muscles in your upper back and chest release and open. Relax your neck and shoulders and allow the relaxation to flow through your arms, and hands.

Begin to feel a tingle in your fingertips and allow any remaining tension in your body to flow out through your fingertips and be released into nothingness.
(pause)

Slowly move your focus to your throat, feeling the muscles of your throat loosen and open, as you think of the soft color of light blue, as this area represents the ability to speak clearly and effectively.

Unclench your teeth, release your jaw muscles, relax the muscles in your cheeks, and just breathe.

(pause)

Let your focus move to your eyes. Now, relax your eye lids and your eye sockets.
(pause)

Gently, move your focus to the spot near the middle of your forehead, between your eyebrows. Relax your eyebrows and all the muscles in your forehead, and think of the color indigo blue, as this area represents foresight, intuition, clarity, and is driven by openness and imagination.
(pause)

Bring your focus to the very top of your head, the crown of your head, feel a tingle there as you relax the muscles in your scalp, and feel it opening as you think of the majestic color of purple, as this area represents Divine connection, and a higher state of consciousness.
(pause)

Now, imagine a bright and beautiful ribbon of crystalline white light coming from above and tethering you to the heavens. Let that light flow to you and through you, enveloping you in a bubble of love and protection.
(pause)

Take a deep breath in and as you exhale allow any remaining tension to be released from your body. Repeating these words in your mind, "peace begins within, peace begins within."
(pause)

• *Guided Meditation*

Let's look at the first four principles.

<u>Step one is honesty</u>.[33] Honesty is the lack of deceit.[34]

In step one, "we admitted we were powerless over alcohol – that our lives had become unmanageable."[35] We must stop deceiving ourselves. We must take a look at ourselves and our lives and be honest. We must continue to be truthful as we take the remaining steps, as well as in our daily affairs. **(pause)**

How are you being more honest in your daily affairs? **(pause)**

Breathe in and breathe out. **(pause)**

<u>Step two is hope</u>[36]. Hope is to cherish a desire with anticipation: to want something to happen or be true, a feeling of optimism.[37]

---

[33] Huff, 2007, 12 Step Companion AA Big Book, Version 2.5.9.6., Updated 2020, [Mobile app] Apple/App Store, © 2007 Dean Huff (Principles)

[34] "Honesty." *Merriam-Webster.com Dictionary*, Merriam-Webster, https://www.merriam-webster.com/dictionary/honesty. Accessed 5 Aug. 2022.

[35] Alcoholics Anonymous Big Book (4th ed.). (2002). Alcoholics Anonymous World Services. (Page 59)

[36] Huff, 2007, 12 Step Companion AA Big Book, Version 2.5.9.6., Updated 2020, [Mobile app] Apple/App Store, © 2007 Dean Huff

[37] "Hope." *Merriam-Webster.com Dictionary*, Merriam-Webster, https://www.merriam-webster.com/dictionary/hope. Accessed 5 Aug. 2022.

In step two, "we came to believe that a Power greater than ourselves could restore us to sanity."[38] We develop an optimism and hope that something good could happen in our life and that a Power greater than ourselves could restore us to sanity. The feeling of hope grows as we progress in the steps and slowly seeps into other areas of our life.
(pause)

How has hope seeped into other areas of your life?
(pause)

Relax and feel the coolness of the air on the tip of your nose as you inhale and the warmth as you exhale.
(pause)

__Step three is faith.__[39] Faith is a firm confidence, belief, and trust.[40]

In step three, "we made a decision to turn our will and our lives over to the care of God as we understood Him."[41] We found a confidence and faith in a Power greater than ourselves and with that faith decided to turn our thoughts and our actions over to the care of God. Seeing how the steps had helped others, we developed a faith that as we

---

[38] Alcoholics Anonymous Big Book (4th ed.). (2002). Alcoholics Anonymous World Services. (Page 59)

[39] Huff, 2007, 12 Step Companion AA Big Book, Version 2.5.9.6., Updated 2020, [Mobile app] Apple/App Store, © 2007 Dean Huff

[40] . "Faith." *Merriam-Webster.com Dictionary*, Merriam-Webster, https://www.merriam-webster.com/dictionary/faith. Accessed 5 Aug. 2022.

[41] Alcoholics Anonymous Big Book (4th ed.). (2002). Alcoholics Anonymous World Services. (Page 59)

move forward, they could work for us too. We start to have faith and confidence in ourselves and eventually in others.

In what areas of your life have you seen your faith grow?
(pause)

Step four is courage.[42] Courage is mental or moral strength to venture, persevere, and withstand fear or difficulty.[43]

In step four, "we made a searching and fearless moral inventory of ourselves."[44] We deepen our mental or moral strength finding courage to make an inventory of ourselves, the good and the bad. Moving forward in the steps and in life, our courage grows, and we can do difficult things and persevere.

How does it feel to have courage?
(pause)

Take a deep breath in and exhale with a sigh.
(pause)

Now, visualize yourself in a variety of moments and experiences where you have practiced honesty, hope, faith and or courage. Take your time.
(pause)

---

[42] Huff, 2007, 12 Step Companion AA Big Book, Version 2.5.9.6., Updated 2020, [Mobile app] Apple/App Store, © 2007 Dean Huff

[43] "Courage." *Merriam-Webster.com Dictionary*, Merriam-Webster, https://www.merriam-webster.com/dictionary/courage. Accessed 5 Aug. 2022.

[44] Alcoholics Anonymous Big Book (4th ed.). (2002). Alcoholics Anonymous World Services. (Page 59)

How does what you visualize make you feel?
(pause)

Have you experienced growth in one principle more than another?
(pause)

How might you grow and deepen these principles within yourself?
(pause)

As we take the steps, the principles become a part of our everyday life. So, whether we are at home, work, or any other place these principles become second nature to us. We practice these principles and understand that no one is perfect. We are not saints.
(pause)

In another meditation, we will look at the principles for steps five, six, seven and eight.
(pause)

Remember, peace begins within. Keep doing the next right thing, one day at a time, one step at a time, one moment at a time.
(pause)

• *Closing*

Start to deepen your breath now and become more aware of your physical body. Take a deep breath in and release it with a sigh. Start to wiggle your fingers and toes, stretch your arms and legs, open your eyes, and come back to the present time and space.

NAMASTE'

Meditation on Recovery Principles for Steps Five, Six, Seven and Eight

What exactly are the principles? We
learn them as we take the steps.
*Step Five is <u>Integrity</u>, Step Six is
<u>Willingness</u>, Step Seven is <u>Humility</u>,
Step Eight is <u>Brotherly Love</u>*[45]

"Surrender is the key to ascending and truly transforming your life. Surrender in each moment as it comes, and you will live a life full of rich moments." (Author Unknown)

This meditation starts with a body scan that assists in relaxation and focus and leads into the portion specific on AA Principles for Steps Five, Six, Seven and Eight.

• *Body Scan*

Now close your eyes, leave all your worries at the door. Allow yourself to relax into the moment. There is only right here, right now.

Clinging to nothing, just be at rest with what is.

---

[45] Huff, 2007, 12 Step Companion AA Big Book, Version 2.5.9.6., Updated 2020, [Mobile app] Apple/App Store, © 2007 Dean Huff

(pause)

Focus on your breathing and the words you hear and if your mind gets distracted, let my voice bring you back and then focus again on your breathing.

Relax now and just breathe.
(pause)

Observe the natural rhythm and flow of your breath.

Take a few moments now, to pay closer attention to it, giving thanks for its presence.
(pause)

Notice the pause at the top of your inhale and again at the bottom of your exhale.
(pause)

Go within, don't think, just breathe.
(pause)

Take a long slow deep breath in and hold it for a moment. Then slowly exhale with a sigh. Allow any tension to melt away.
(pause)

Feel the coolness of the air on the tip of your nose as you inhale and the warmth of the breath as you exhale.
(pause)

Feel the rise of your chest and abdomen on each inhale and the fall on every exhale. As you exhale, let go of any stress or tension, see it floating away, as you gradually relax more deeply with each breath.

(pause)

Grounding ourselves helps us to shed any feelings of anxiety, restlessness, or fear that may be lingering in body or mind.

So, take a few minutes now to feel grounded and simply connected to the earth. Notice the breath as it nourishes every cell of your body.

(pause)

Focused breathing allows your mind to slow down. On your own really focus on your next three breathes as you gently inhale and exhale.

(pause)

Feel the energy that comes from the earth, its strength and stability. Let this energy ground you. Feel that energy come through the souls of your feet, like a breeze flowing through and over your entire body.

(pause)

Now, feeling that grounded energy, begin to feel a tingle in the tips of your toes and the souls of your feet, know that you are safe, stable, supported and loved.

(pause)

Now, gently bring your focus to your ankles, your calves, your thighs, feeling those muscles relax, as you feel yourself sinking into the surface you are resting upon.

(pause)

Breathe in and breathe out.

Move your focus to your buttocks... and hips, release any tension you may be feeling and allow yourself to drift into a state of deep relaxation.

(pause)

Focus on the base of your spine, relaxing the muscles in your lower back, feel a warmth and think of the strong color red, as this area represents stability, safety, and security.

(pause)

Now allow that feeling of warmth and relaxation to move to your lower abdominal muscles, just below your belly button, and think of the warm color orange, as this area represents creativity and sexual energies.

(pause)

Feel your body relaxing with each breath you take.

(pause)

Move your focus to your upper abdominal muscles, just above your belly button, relax those muscles and feel a warmth and relaxation as you think of the vibrant color

yellow, as this area represents will-power, self-esteem, pleasure, and personal responsibility.

(pause)

Breathe in God's love and peace and breathe out all resistance.

(pause)

Now feel the warmth and relaxation move slowly and gently to your heart center, in the middle of your chest and about two inches in, and think of a beautiful color of green, as this area represents self-love, our love for others and governs our relationships.

(pause)

Feel yourself becoming deeper and deeper relaxed, your breath will assist you.

(pause)

Feel the muscles in your upper back and chest release and open. Relax your neck and shoulders and allow the relaxation to flow through your arms, and hands.

Begin to feel a tingle in your fingertips and allow any remaining tension in your body to flow out through your fingertips and be released into nothingness.

(pause)

Slowly move your focus to your throat, feeling the muscles of your throat loosen and open, as you think of the soft

color of light blue, as this area represents the ability to speak clearly and effectively.

Unclench your teeth, release your jaw muscles, relax the muscles in your cheeks, and just breathe.
(pause)

Let your focus move to your eyes. Now, relax your eye lids and your eye sockets.
(pause)

Gently, move your focus to the spot near the middle of your forehead, between your eyebrows. Relax your eyebrows and all the muscles in your forehead, and think of the color indigo blue, as this area represents foresight, intuition, clarity, and is driven by openness and imagination.
(pause)

Bring your focus to the very top of your head, the crown of your head, feel a tingle there as you relax the muscles in your scalp, and feel it opening as you think of the majestic color of purple, as this area represents Divine connection, and a higher state of consciousness.
(pause)

Now, imagine a bright and beautiful ribbon of crystalline white light coming from above and tethering you to the heavens. Let that light flow to you and through you, enveloping you in a bubble of love and protection.
(pause)

Take a deep breath in and as you exhale allow any remaining tension to be released from your body. Repeating these words in your mind, "peace begins within, peace begins within." **(pause)**

• *Guided Meditation*

Let's look at the principles for steps five through eight.

<u>Step five is integrity.</u>[46] Integrity is soundness of moral character, honesty, honorable intentions.[47]

In step five, "we admit to God, to ourselves and to another human being the exact nature of our wrongs."[48] These wrongs are listed in our fourth step inventory. Being completely honest, open, and willing, and leaving nothing out of our discussion is vital for recovery. We demonstrate integrity by holding ourselves accountable and owning up to our shortcomings.

Do you hold yourself accountable to being honest and honorable in all your affairs? **(pause)**

Remember, peace begins within. **(pause)**

---

[46] Huff, 2007, 12 Step Companion AA Big Book, Version 2.5.9.6., Updated 2020, [Mobile app] Apple/App Store, © 2007 Dean Huff

[47] "Integrity." *Merriam-Webster.com Dictionary*, Merriam-Webster, https://www.merriam-webster.com/dictionary/integrity. Accessed 5 Aug. 2022.

[48] Alcoholics Anonymous Big Book (4th ed.). (2002). Alcoholics Anonymous World Services. (Page 59)

<u>Step six is willingness.</u>[49] Willingness is the quality or state of being prepared to do something; of or relating to the power of choosing; desire[50].

In step six, "we were entirely ready to have God remove all these defects of character."[51] These defects of character or survival skills that no longer serve us, were revealed in the previous step. In the Big Book, it says more will be revealed. Therefore, we need to keep the desire to allow God to remove undesirable behavior in the forefront of our minds.

(pause)

How have you demonstrated your desire and willingness to allow your Higher Power to work in your recovery and your daily life?

(pause)

Take a deep breath in and exhale with a sigh.

(pause)

<u>Step seven is humility.</u>[52] Humility is having or showing a moderate or humble estimate of one's merits

---

[49] Huff, 2007, 12 Step Companion AA Big Book, Version 2.5.9.6., Updated 2020, [Mobile app] Apple/App Store, © 2007 Dean Huff

[50] "Willing." *Merriam-Webster.com Dictionary*, Merriam-Webster, https://www.merriam-webster.com/dictionary/willing. Accessed 5 Aug. 2022.

[51] Alcoholics Anonymous Big Book (4th ed.). (2002). Alcoholics Anonymous World Services. (Page 59)

[52] Huff, 2007, 12 Step Companion AA Big Book, Version 2.5.9.6., Updated 2020, [Mobile app] Apple/App Store, © 2007 Dean Huff

or importance, free from vanity, egotism, boastfulness, or great pretensions.[53]

In step seven, "we humbly asked our Higher Power to remove our shortcomings."[54] We learn to find balance, not to be full of pride or self-pity.

In our daily lives we can demonstrate humility by being God centered and not self-centered. Being mindful of others, listening, reviewing your actions against the language of pride, and showing gratitude.

Are you consciously developing an attitude of humility in all areas of your life?
(pause)

Breathe in and breathe out.
(pause)

Step eight is brotherly love.[55] Brotherly love is a kindly and lenient attitude toward people.[56]

In step eight, "we made a list of all persons we had harmed and became willing to make amends to them all."[57] In this

---

[53] "Humility." *Merriam-Webster.com Dictionary*, Merriam-Webster, https://www.merriam-webster.com/dictionary/humility. Accessed 5 Aug. 2022.

[54] Alcoholics Anonymous Big Book (4th ed.). (2002). Alcoholics Anonymous World Services. (Page 59)

[55] Huff, 2007, 12 Step Companion AA Big Book, Version 2.5.9.6., Updated 2020, [Mobile app] Apple/App Store, © 2007 Dean Huff

[56] "Brotherly Love." https://www.vocabulary.com/dictionary/brotherly%20love. Accessed 5 Aug. 2022

[57] Alcoholics Anonymous Big Book (4th ed.). (2002). Alcoholics Anonymous World Services. (Page 59)

step, we develop brotherly love when we are confronted with the knowledge that we are responsible for another's suffering and feel motivated to make amends and relieve that suffering.

How are you showing brotherly love, concern, and compassion towards others in your daily affairs?
(pause)

Take a deep breath in and exhale with a sigh.
(pause)

Now, visualize yourself in a variety of moments and experiences where you have practiced integrity, willingness, humility and or brotherly love. Take your time.
(pause)

How does it make you feel?
(pause)

Have you experienced growth in one principle more than another?
(pause)

How might you grow and deepen these principles within yourself?
(pause)

As we take the steps, the principles become a part of our everyday life. So, whether we are at home, work, or any other place these principles become second nature to us.

We practice these principles and understand that no one is perfect. We are not saints.
(pause)

In another meditation, we will look at the principles for steps nine, ten, eleven and twelve.
(pause)

Remember, peace begins within. Keep doing the next right thing, one day at a time, one step at a time, one moment at a time.
(pause)

• *Closing*

Start to deepen your breath now and become more aware of your physical body. Take a deep breath in and release it with a sigh. Start to wiggle your fingers and toes, stretch your arms and legs, open your eyes, and come back to the present time and space.

NAMASTE'

Meditation on Recovery Principles for Steps Nine, Ten, Eleven and Twelve

What exactly are the principles? We
learn them as we take the steps.

Step Nine is <u>Justice</u>, Step Ten <u>is Perseverance</u>,
Step Eleven is <u>Spirituality</u>,
Step Twelve is <u>Service</u>[58]

"Surrender is the key to ascending and truly transforming your life. Surrender in each moment as it comes, and you will live a life full of rich moments." (Author Unknown)

This meditation starts with a body scan that assists in relaxation and focus and leads into the portion specific on AA Principles for Steps Nine, Ten, Eleven and Twelve.

• *Body Scan*

Now close your eyes, leave all your worries at the door. Allow yourself to relax into the moment. There is only right here, right now.

---

[58] Huff, 2007, 12 Step Companion AA Big Book, Version 2.5.9.6., Updated 2020, [Mobile app] Apple/App Store, © 2007 Dean Huff

Clinging to nothing, just be at rest with what is.
(pause)

Focus on your breathing and the words you hear and if your mind gets distracted, let my voice bring you back and then focus again on your breathing.

Relax now and just breathe.
(pause)

Observe the natural rhythm and flow of your breath.

Take a few moments now, to pay closer attention to it, giving thanks for its presence.
(pause)

Notice the pause at the top of your inhale and again at the bottom of your exhale.
(pause)

Go within, don't think, just breathe.
(pause)

Take a long slow deep breath in and hold it for a moment. Then slowly exhale with a sigh. Allow any tension to melt away.
(pause)

Feel the coolness of the air on the tip of your nose as you inhale and the warmth of the breath as you exhale.
(pause)

Feel the rise of your chest and abdomen on each inhale and the fall on every exhale. As you exhale, let go of any stress or tension, see it floating away, as you gradually relax more deeply with each breath.

(pause)

Grounding ourselves helps us to shed any feelings of anxiety, restlessness, or fear that may be lingering in body or mind.

So, take a few minutes now to feel grounded and simply connected to the earth. Notice the breath as it nourishes every cell of your body.

(pause)

Focused breathing allows your mind to slow down. On your own really focus on your next three breathes as you gently inhale and exhale.

(pause)

Feel the energy that comes from the earth, its strength and stability. Let this energy ground you. Feel that energy come through the souls of your feet, like a breeze flowing through and over your entire body.

(pause)

Now, feeling that grounded energy, begin to feel a tingle in the tips of your toes and the souls of your feet, know that you are safe, stable, supported and loved.

(pause)

Now, gently bring your focus to your ankles, your calves, your thighs, feeling those muscles relax, as you feel yourself sinking into the surface you are resting upon.
(pause)

Breathe in and breathe out.

Move your focus to your buttocks… and hips, release any tension you may be feeling and allow yourself to drift into a state of deep relaxation.
(pause)

Focus on the base of your spine, relaxing the muscles in your lower back, feel a warmth and think of the strong color red, as this area represents stability, safety, and security.
(pause)

Now allow that feeling of warmth and relaxation to move to your lower abdominal muscles, just below your belly button, and think of the warm color orange, as this area represents creativity and sexual energies.
(pause)

Feel your body relaxing with each breath you take.
(pause)

Move your focus to your upper abdominal muscles, just above your belly button, relax those muscles and feel a warmth and relaxation as you think of the vibrant color

yellow, as this area represents will-power, self-esteem, pleasure, and personal responsibility.
(pause)

Breathe in God's love and peace and breathe out all resistance.
(pause)

Now feel the warmth and relaxation move slowly and gently to your heart center, in the middle of your chest and about two inches in, and think of a beautiful color of green, as this area represents self-love, our love for others and governs our relationships.
(pause)

Feel yourself becoming deeper and deeper relaxed, your breath will assist you.
(pause)

Feel the muscles in your upper back and chest release and open. Relax your neck and shoulders and allow the relaxation to flow through your arms, and hands.

Begin to feel a tingle in your fingertips and allow any remaining tension in your body to flow out through your fingertips and be released into nothingness.
(pause)

Slowly move your focus to your throat, feeling the muscles of your throat loosen and open, as you think of the soft

color of light blue, as this area represents the ability to speak clearly and effectively.

Unclench your teeth, release your jaw muscles, relax the muscles in your cheeks, and just breathe.
(pause)

Let your focus move to your eyes. Now, relax your eye lids and your eye sockets.
(pause)

Gently, move your focus to the spot near the middle of your forehead, between your eyebrows. Relax your eyebrows and all the muscles in your forehead, and think of the color indigo blue, as this area represents foresight, intuition, clarity, and is driven by openness and imagination.
(pause)

Bring your focus to the very top of your head, the crown of your head, feel a tingle there as you relax the muscles in your scalp, and feel it opening as you think of the majestic color of purple, as this area represents Divine connection, and a higher state of consciousness.
(pause)

Now, imagine a bright and beautiful ribbon of crystalline white light coming from above and tethering you to the heavens. Let that light flow to you and through you, enveloping you in a bubble of love and protection.
(pause)

Take a deep breath in and as you exhale allow any remaining tension to be released from your body. Repeating these words in your mind, "peace begins within, peace begins within."
(pause)

• *Guided Meditation*

Let's look at the last four principles.

Step nine is justice.[59] Justice is moral rightness. We are called to take action and confront evil, to care for the vulnerable, and to make right that which is wrong.[60]

In step nine, "we made direct amends to such people wherever possible, except when to do so would injure them or others."[61] This is where we learn to make right, that which is wrong. Making amends and moving forward to treat others fairly and with moral rightness in our daily affairs is freeing.

Are you mindful of how you treat others?
(pause)

---

[59] Huff, 2007, 12 Step Companion AA Big Book, Version 2.5.9.6., Updated 2020, [Mobile app] Apple/App Store, © 2007 Dean Huff

[60] "Justice" https://sharedhope.org/2018/06/04/biblical-justice-and-social-justice/#:~:text=As%20we%20look%20at%20the,right%20that%20which%20is%20wrong. Accessed 5 Aug. 2022

[61] Alcoholics Anonymous Big Book (4th ed.). (2002). Alcoholics Anonymous World Services. (Page 59)

Breathe in and breathe out.
(pause)

<u>Step ten is perseverance.</u>[62] Perseverance is continued effort to do or achieve something despite difficulties, failure, or opposition.[63]

In step ten, "we continued to take personal inventory and when we were wrong promptly admitted it."[64] Remember, we are not saints. However, we do continue to try and do the next right thing. When we fail, we pick ourselves up and resume our efforts.

Think of a moment where you persevered and overcame a challenging time in your life and how you can continue this growth now, in you daily life.
(pause)

Peace begins within, peace begins within.
(pause)

<u>Step eleven is Spirituality.</u>[65] Spirituality is the recognition of a feeling, sense, or belief that there is something greater

---

[62] Huff, 2007, 12 Step Companion AA Big Book, Version 2.5.9.6., Updated 2020, [Mobile app] Apple/App Store, © 2007 Dean Huff

[63] "Perseverance." *Merriam-Webster.com Dictionary*, Merriam-Webster, https://www.merriam-webster.com/dictionary/perseverance. Accessed 5 Aug. 2022.

[64] Alcoholics Anonymous Big Book (4th ed.). (2002). Alcoholics Anonymous World Services. (Page 59)

[65] Huff, 2007, 12 Step Companion AA Big Book, Version 2.5.9.6., Updated 2020, [Mobile app] Apple/App Store, © 2007 Dean Huff

than myself, and that our soul is connected to something divine or cosmic.[66]

In step eleven, "we sought through prayer and meditation to improve our conscious contact with God as we understood Him, praying only for the knowledge of His Will for us and the power to carry that out."[67] Spirituality is often a new idea, and it develops over time. There is a peace that is beyond understanding when spirituality becomes a part of your daily affairs.

What is your spiritual practice?
(pause)

Relax, breathe, and go within.
(pause)

Step twelve is service.[68] Service is an act of helpful activity; help; aid.[69]

In step twelve, "having had a spiritual awakening as the result of these steps, we tried to carry this message to alcoholics, and to practice these principles in all our affairs."[70] There are others who came before us and gave

---

[66] "Spirituality" © Maya Spencer 2012, What is spirituality? A personal exploration Dr Maya Spencer, Royal College of Psychiatrist. Accessed 5 Aug. 2022

[67] Alcoholics Anonymous Big Book (4th ed.). (2002). Alcoholics Anonymous World Services. (Page 59)

[68] Huff, 2007, 12 Step Companion AA Big Book, Version 2.5.9.6., Updated 2020, [Mobile app] Apple/App Store, © 2007 Dean Huff

[69] "Service." *Merriam-Webster.com Dictionary*, Merriam-Webster, https://www.merriam-webster.com/dictionary/service. Accessed 5 Aug. 2022.

[70] Alcoholics Anonymous Big Book (4th ed.). (2002). Alcoholics Anonymous World Services. (Page 60)

freely of what was given to them. They helped us through the steps. We now see, through example, that service is how we share the steps and our own spiritual awakening as well as give back to everyone. We lose interest in ourselves and gain interest in our fellows.

How are you being helpful and of service to others in your life?
(pause)

Now, visualize yourself in a variety of moments and experiences where you have practiced justice, perseverance, spirituality and or service. Take your time.
(pause)

How does it make you feel?
(pause)

Have you experienced growth in one area more than another?
(pause)

How might you grow and deepen these principles within yourself?
(pause)

Breathe in and breathe out.
(pause)

As we take the steps, the principles become a part of our everyday life. So, whether we are at home, work, or any other place these principles become second nature to us.

We practice these principles and understand that no one is perfect. We are not saints.

(pause)

Remember, peace begins within. Keep doing the next right thing, one day at a time, one step at a time, one moment at a time.

(pause)

• *Closing*

Start to deepen your breath now and become more aware of your physical body. Take a deep breath in and release it with a sigh. Start to wiggle your fingers and toes, stretch your arms and legs, open your eyes, and come back to the present time and space.

NAMASTE'

The Principles and The Steps

What exactly are the principles? We
learn them as we take the steps.

*Step One is <u>Honesty</u>, Step Two is <u>Hope</u>, Step
Three is <u>Faith</u>, Step Four is <u>Courage</u>.*

*Step Five is <u>Integrity</u>, Step Six is
<u>Willingness</u>, Step Seven is <u>Humility</u>,*

Step Eight is <u>Brotherly Love</u>, Step Nine is <u>Justice</u>,

*Step Ten is <u>Perseverance</u>, Step Eleven is
<u>Spirituality</u>, Step Twelve is <u>Service</u>[71]*

<u>Step one is honesty</u>. Honesty is the lack of deceit.[72]

In step one, "We admitted we were powerless over
alcohol – that our lives had become unmanageable."[73] We
must stop deceiving ourselves. We must be honest that we
are powerless over alcohol and that our lives have become

---

[71] Huff, 2007, 12 Step Companion AA Big Book, Version 2.5.9.6., Updated 2020, [Mobile
app] Apple/App Store, © 2007 Dean Huff

[72] "Honesty." *Merriam-Webster.com Dictionary*, Merriam-Webster, https://www.merriam-
webster.com/dictionary/honesty. Accessed 5 Aug. 2022.

[73] Alcoholics Anonymous Big Book (4th ed.). (2002). Alcoholics Anonymous World
Services (Page 59)

unmanageable. We must continue to be truthful as we take the remaining steps, as well as in our daily affairs.

Step two is hope.[74] Hope is grounds for believing that something good may happen, a feeling of optimism.[75]

In step two, "Came to believe that a Power greater than ourselves could restore us to sanity."[76] We develop an optimism and hope that something good could happen in our life and that a power greater than ourselves could restore us to sanity. The feeling of hope grows as we progress in the steps and slowly seeps into other areas of our life.

Step three is faith.[77] Faith is a firm confidence, belief, and trust.[78]

In step three, "Made a decision to turn our will and our lives over to the care of God as we understood Him."[79] We found a confidence and a faith in a power greater than ourselves and with that faith, made a decision to turn our will and our life over to the care of God as we understood God. Seeing how the steps had helped others, we developed a faith that as we move forward, that they could work for

---

[74] Huff, 2007, 12 Step Companion AA Big Book, Version 2.5.9.6., Updated 2020, [Mobile app] Apple/App Store, © 2007 Dean Huff

[75] "Hope." *Merriam-Webster.com Dictionary*, Merriam-Webster, https://www.merriam-webster.com/dictionary/hope. Accessed 5 Aug. 2022.

[76] Alcoholics Anonymous Big Book (4th ed.). (2002). Alcoholics Anonymous World Services (Page 59)

[77] Huff, 2007, 12 Step Companion AA Big Book

[78] "Faith." *Merriam-Webster.com Dictionary*, Merriam-Webster, https://www.merriam-webster.com/dictionary/faith. Accessed 5 Aug. 2022.

[79] Alcoholics Anonymous Big Book (4th ed.). (2002). Alcoholics Anonymous World Services (Page 59

us too. We start to have faith and confidence in ourselves and eventually in others.

Step four is courage.[80] Courage is mental or moral strength to venture, persevere, and withstand fear or difficulty.[81]

In step four, "Made a searching and fearless moral inventory of ourselves."[82] We deepen our mental or moral strength finding courage to make a searching and fearless moral inventory of ourselves. Moving forward in the steps and in life, our courage grows, and we can do difficult things and persevere.

Step five is integrity.[83] Integrity is soundness of moral character, honesty, honorable intentions.[84]

In step five, "Admitted to God, to ourselves and to another human being the exact nature of our wrongs."[85] These wrongs are listed in our fourth step inventory. Being completely honest, open, and willing, and leaving nothing out of our discussion is vital for recovery. We demonstrate integrity by holding ourselves accountable and owning up to our shortcomings.

[80] Huff, 2007, 12 Step Companion AA Big Book, Version 2.5.9.6., Updated 2020, [Mobile app] Apple/App Store, © 2007 Dean Huff

[81] "Courage." *Merriam-Webster.com Dictionary*, Merriam-Webster, https://www.merriam-webster.com/dictionary/courage. Accessed 5 Aug. 2022.

[82] Alcoholics Anonymous Big Book (4th ed.)

[83] Huff, 2007, 12 Step Companion AA Big Book, Version 2.5.9.6., Updated 2020, [Mobile app] Apple/App Store, © 2007 Dean Huff

[84] "Integrity." *Merriam-Webster.com Dictionary*, Merriam-Webster, https://www.merriam-webster.com/dictionary/integrity. Accessed 5 Aug. 2022.

[85] Alcoholics Anonymous Big Book (4th ed.). (2002). Alcoholics Anonymous World Services (Page 59)

Step six is willingness.[86] Willingness is the quality or state of being prepared to do something; of or relating to the will or power of choosing; desire.[87]

In step six, "Were entirely ready to have God remove all these defects of character."[88] These defects of character or survival skills that no longer serve us, were revealed in the previous step. In the Big Book, it says more will be revealed. Therefore, we need to keep the desire to allow God to remove undesirable behavior in the forefront of our minds.

Step seven is humility. [89] Humility is having or showing a moderate or humble estimate of one's merits, importance, etc.; free from vanity, egotism, boastfulness, or great pretensions.[90]

In step seven, "Humbly asked our Higher Power to remove our shortcomings."[91] We learn to find balance, not to be full of pride or self-pity. In our daily lives we can demonstrate humility by being God centered and not self–centered. Being mindful of others, listening, reviewing your actions against the language of pride, and showing gratitude.

---

[86] Huff, 2007, 12 Step Companion AA Big Book,

[87] "Willing." *Merriam-Webster.com Dictionary*, Merriam-Webster, https://www.merriam-webster.com/dictionary/willing. Accessed 5 Aug. 2022.

[88] Alcoholics Anonymous Big Book (4th ed.). (2002). Alcoholics Anonymous World Services (Page 59)

[89] Huff, 2007, 12 Step Companion AA Big Book, Version 2.5.9.6., Updated 2020, [Mobile app] Apple/App Store, © 2007 Dean Huff

[90] "Humility." *Merriam-Webster.com Dictionary*, Merriam-Webster, https://www.merriam-webster.com/dictionary/humility. Accessed 5 Aug. 2022.

[91] Alcoholics Anonymous Big Book (4th ed.).

<u>Step eight is brotherly love.</u>[92] Brotherly love is compassion toward one's fellow humans and concern for the sufferings or misfortunes of others.[93]

In step eight, "Made a list of all persons we had harmed and became willing to make amends to them all."[94] In this step, we develop brotherly love when we are confronted with the knowledge that we are responsible for another's suffering and feel motivated to relieve that suffering.

<u>Step nine is justice.</u>[95] Justice is moral rightness, fair treatment and to make right that which is wrong.[96]

In step nine, "Made direct amends to such people wherever possible, except when to do so would injure them or others."[97] This is where we learn to make right, that which is wrong. Making amends and moving forward to treat others fairly and with moral rightness in our daily affairs is freeing.

---

[92] Huff, 2007, 12 Step Companion AA Big Book, Version 2.5.9.6., Updated 2020, [Mobile app] Apple/App Store, © 2007 Dean Huff

[93] "Brotherly Love." https://www.vocabulary.com/dictionary/brotherly%20love. Accessed 5 Aug. 2022

[94] Alcoholics Anonymous Big Book (4th ed.). (2002). Alcoholics Anonymous World Services (Page 59)

[95] Huff, 2007, 12 Step Companion AA Big Book

[96] "Justice" https://sharedhope.org/2018/06/04/biblical-justice-and-social-justice/#:~:text=As%20we%20look%20at%20the,right%20that%20which%20is%20wrong. Accessed 5 Aug. 2022

[97] Alcoholics Anonymous Big Book (4th ed.).

Step ten is perseverance.[98] Perseverance is continued effort to do or achieve something despite difficulties, failure, or opposition.[99]

In step ten, "Continued to take personal inventory and when we were wrong promptly admitted it."[100] Remember, we are not saints. However, we do continue to try and do the next right thing. When we fail, we pick ourselves up and resume our efforts.

Step eleven is spirituality.[101] Spirituality is the recognition of a feeling, sense, or belief that there is something greater than myself, and that our soul is connected to something divine or cosmic.[102]

In step eleven, "Sought through prayer and meditation to improve our conscious contact with God as we understood Him, praying only for the knowledge of His well for us and the power to carry that out."[103] Spirituality is often a new idea, and it is develops over time. There is a peace that is beyond understanding when spirituality becomes a part of your daily affairs.

---

[98] Huff, 2007, 12 Step Companion AA Big Book, Version 2.5.9.6., Updated 2020, [Mobile app] Apple/App Store, © 2007 Dean Huff

[99] "Perseverance." *Merriam-Webster.com Dictionary*, Merriam-Webster, https://www.merriam-webster.com/dictionary/perseverance. Accessed 5 Aug. 2022.

[100] Alcoholics Anonymous Big Book (4th ed.). (2002). Alcoholics Anonymous World Services (Page 59)

[101] Huff, 2007, 12 Step Companion AA Big Book,

[102] "Spirituality" © Maya Spencer 2012, What is spirituality? A personal exploration Dr Maya Spencer, Royal College of Psychiatrist. Accessed 5 Aug. 2022

[103] Alcoholics Anonymous Big Book (4th ed.). (2002). Alcoholics Anonymous World Services (Page 59)

Step twelve is service.[104] Service is an act of helpful activity; help; aid.[105]

In step twelve, "Having had a spiritual awakening as the results of these steps, we tried to carry this message to the alcoholic, and to practice these principles in all our affairs."[106] There are others who came before us and gave freely of what was given to them. They helped us through the steps. We now see, through example, that service is how we share the steps and our own spiritual awakening as well as give back to everyone. We lose interest in ourselves and gain interest in our fellows.

[104] Huff, 2007, 12 Step Companion AA Big Book, Version 2.5.9.6., Updated 2020, [Mobile app] Apple/App Store, © 2007 Dean Huff

[105] "Service." *Merriam-Webster.com Dictionary*, Merriam-Webster, https://www.merriam-webster.com/dictionary/service. Accessed 5 Aug. 2022.

[106] Alcoholics Anonymous Big Book (4th ed.). (2002). Alcoholics Anonymous World Services (Page 60)

PART THREE

Personal Growth

Meditation for when you need to "PAUSE"

When agitated, angry, irritable, or discontent,
we pause and then we pray.

Surrender is the key to ascending and truly transforming
your life. Surrender in each moment as it comes, and you
will live a life full of rich moments. (Author Unknown)

*This meditation starts with a body scan that assists
in relaxation and focus and leads into the portion
specific on when you need to "PAUSE".*

- ### *Body Scan*

Now close your eyes, leave all your worries at the door.
Allow yourself to relax into the moment. There is only
right here, right now.

Clinging to nothing, just be at rest with what is.
(pause)

Focus on your breathing and the words you hear and if
your mind gets distracted, let my voice bring you back and
then focus again on your breathing.

Relax now and just breathe.
(pause)

Observe the natural rhythm and flow of your breath.

Take a few moments now, to pay closer attention to it, giving thanks for its presence.
(pause)

Notice the pause at the top of your inhale and again at the bottom of your exhale.
(pause)

Go within, don't think, just breathe.
(pause)

Take a long slow deep breath in and hold it for a moment. Then slowly exhale with a sigh. Allow any tension to melt away.
(pause)

Feel the coolness of the air on the tip of your nose as you inhale and the warmth of the breath as you exhale.
(pause)

Feel the rise of your chest and abdomen on each inhale and the fall on every exhale. As you exhale, let go of any stress or tension, see it floating away, as you gradually relax more deeply with each breath.
(pause)

Grounding ourselves helps us to shed any feelings of anxiety, restlessness, or fear that may be lingering in body or mind.

So, take a few minutes now to feel grounded and simply connected to the earth. Notice the breath as it nourishes every cell of your body.
(pause)

Focused breathing allows your mind to slow down. On your own really focus on your next three breathes as you gently inhale and exhale.
(pause)

Feel the energy that comes from the earth, its strength and stability. Let this energy ground you. Feel that energy come through the souls of your feet, like a breeze flowing through and over your entire body.
(pause)

Now, feeling that grounded energy, begin to feel a tingle in the tips of your toes and the souls of your feet, know that you are safe, stable, supported and loved.
(pause)

Now, gently bring your focus to your ankles, your calves, your thighs, feeling those muscles relax, as you feel yourself sinking into the surface you are resting upon.
(pause)

Breathe in and breathe out.

Move your focus to your buttocks… and hips, release any tension you may be feeling and allow yourself to drift into a state of deep relaxation.

(pause)

Focus on the base of your spine, relaxing the muscles in your lower back, feel a warmth and think of the strong color red, as this area represents stability, safety, and security.

(pause)

Now allow that feeling of warmth and relaxation to move to your lower abdominal muscles, just below your belly button, and think of the warm color orange, as this area represents creativity and sexual energies.

(pause)

Feel your body relaxing with each breath you take.

(pause)

Move your focus to your upper abdominal muscles, just above your belly button, relax those muscles and feel a warmth and relaxation as you think of the vibrant color yellow, as this area represents will-power, self-esteem, pleasure, and personal responsibility.

(pause)

Breathe in God's love and peace and breathe out all resistance.

(pause)

Now feel the warmth and relaxation move slowly and gently to your heart center, in the middle of your chest

and about two inches in, and think of a beautiful color of green, as this area represents self-love, our love for others and governs our relationships.

(pause)

Feel yourself becoming deeper and deeper relaxed, your breath will assist you.

(pause)

Feel the muscles in your upper back and chest release and open. Relax your neck and shoulders and allow the relaxation to flow through your arms, and hands.

Begin to feel a tingle in your fingertips and allow any remaining tension in your body to flow out through your fingertips and be released into nothingness.

(pause)

Slowly move your focus to your throat, feeling the muscles of your throat loosen and open, as you think of the soft color of light blue, as this area represents the ability to speak clearly and effectively.

Unclench your teeth, release your jaw muscles, relax the muscles in your cheeks, and just breathe.

(pause)

Let your focus move to your eyes. Now, relax your eye lids and your eye sockets.

(pause)

Gently, move your focus to the spot near the middle of your forehead, between your eyebrows. Relax your eyebrows and all the muscles in your forehead, and think of the color indigo blue, as this area represents foresight, intuition, clarity, and is driven by openness and imagination.
(pause)

Bring your focus to the very top of your head, the crown of your head, feel a tingle there as you relax the muscles in your scalp, and feel it opening as you think of the majestic color of purple, as this area represents Divine connection, and a higher state of consciousness.
(pause)

Now, imagine a bright and beautiful ribbon of crystalline white light coming from above and tethering you to the heavens. Let that light flow to you and through you, enveloping you in a bubble of love and protection.
(pause)

Take a deep breath in and as you exhale allow any remaining tension to be released from your body. Repeating these words in your mind, "peace begins within, peace begins within."
(pause)

- ### *Guided Meditation*

In all times of emotional disturbance or indecision, we can pause, ask for quiet, and in the stillness simply say: "God grant me the serenity to accept the things I cannot change, courage to change the things I can, and wisdom to know the difference. Thy will, not mine, be done."[107]

(pause)

The root of our problems was the habit of holding onto unhealthy resentments and fears. We all have emotions and sometimes, "*feeling*" them is difficult.

(pause)

The act of surrender in recovery is a willingness to give up the fight, we allow ourselves to feel emotions that alcohol used to numb. Emotions such as fear, pain, insecurities, and lack of control. The question is, "how do we surrender, how do we become willing to give up the fight?" We pause, and when we pause, we pray!

"We pause, when agitated or doubtful, and ask/pray for the right thought or action, "Thy will, not mine, be done."[108]

(pause)

When you pause to pray, be still, breathe, relax, and meditate, opening your heart and mind to "hear" or "feel" the guidance of your Higher Power. You might ask yourself, "What is my part in this?", "When have I behaved in this same way?", "Do I need to make an amends?"

(pause)

---

[107] Alcoholics Anonymous World Services, Inc. (1989). *Twelve steps and Twelve Traditions.* Alcoholics Anonymous World Services. (pp.40-41)

[108] Alcoholics Anonymous Big Book (4th ed.). (2002). Alcoholics Anonymous World Services. (Pg. 87)

"Does this need to be said, does it need to be said by me, does it need to be said by me right now?"
(pause)

"How important is this in the big picture of life?", "Am I hungry, angry, lonely, or tired?" "Is holding on to this feeling helping or hurting me?"
(pause)

God, "How or What do I pray for this person, place, or thing that is disturbing me?"
(pause)

"Is my serenity more important?" "Am I really just upset with myself?" "Do I need to call my sponsor or go to a meeting?" "What is the next right step?"
(pause)

Ignoring feelings is no longer an option. It's time to come to acceptance, to deal with irritability, agitation, discontent, or doubt in a healthy, productive way.
(pause)

Irritability, agitation, or doubt are normal emotions, and there is nothing wrong with having feelings – you are human, after all. You have the power to choose how to deal with these emotions that you are experiencing. You pause and ask your Higher Power for help in managing your emotional responses.
(pause)

You might start to worry about the future or think about the past—it's normal for your mind to wander. Some feelings and thoughts might be very distressing but do your best to observe your feelings and not judge. Just allow yourself to feel any anger, irritability, agitation, discontent, or doubt that you may be experiencing. Only noticing or observing this feeling, but not reacting. Emotions are neither right nor wrong. They just are.

(pause)

Now, take a deep breath in. Hold for a moment, and now breathe out with a sigh.

(pause)

Allow your breathing to return to a gentle natural rhythm, slowly.... deeply.... and let your body relax.

(pause)

Turn your attention again to how you feel.

Where in your physical body is that feeling of anger, irritability, agitation, discontent, or doubt stored? Some people notice that they tighten their shoulders, others may notice clenched fists or tight jaws, it might be a feeling in the pit of your stomach, or others may hold their breath. Where do you feel these feelings in your body?

(pause)

Starting with your hands and arms, first tighten your hands into fists. Feel the tension in your hands and arms. Hold.... tighter.... tighter.... and......... now release. Let go, allowing

your hands and arms to be relaxed, loose, and limp. Notice the difference between tension and relaxation. Many of these physical symptoms are uncomfortable. Some of these symptoms can be relieved just by relaxing your muscles.
(pause)

Focus on those areas where you hold on to your emotions. Now, imagine those physical symptoms becoming more relaxed and your breathing slowing down, and let the tension float out of those areas of your body.
(pause)

Search your body now, for any remaining areas of tension. Relax each area that feels tense. Scan your body from head to toe, relaxing each part of your body.
(pause)

Take note of how you are feeling now. Physically. Emotionally.
(pause)

That peaceful easy feeling is you surrendering, you can choose to pause, give it to your Higher Power, relax, and deal with your feelings in a healthy way.
(pause)

You might want to pause and, in your mind, say something like, "With the help of my Higher Power, I can choose the way I respond." Or "I am okay, right here, right now."
(pause)

You know emotions come and go. Feelings of irritability, agitation and doubt come and go, they will not last forever. As it is said, "This Too Shall Pass."
(pause)

You do not have to keep your emotions inside... you can choose how to express them. You can let feelings out by meditating and breathing deeply.... breathing in relaxation and breathing out all your tension.... "Letting Go and Letting God", with each breath.
(pause)

There are other ways to process emotions. You can meditate, do physical exercise, journal, write a gratitude list, talk to someone you trust.
(pause)

After the emotion has decreased and you feel calmer, you might want to address the situation that was upsetting you by taking positive action to change it, by speaking to the person you were upset with, or you may just choose to let the situation go. You have paused and now can choose whatever option seems best.
(pause)

You have the right to feel a range of emotions, and you can choose to express these emotions in healthy ways. Appreciate that you are growing and learning new ways of expressing how you feel, with the help of your High Power.
(pause)

Take a deep breath in, and out.
(pause)

Remember, peace begins within.
(pause)

• *Closing*

Start to deepen your breath now and become more aware of your physical body. Take a deep breath in and release it with a sigh. Start to wiggle your fingers and toes, stretch your arms and legs, open your eyes, and come back to the present time and space.

NAMASTE'

Meditation To Be Still and Listen

"Surrender is the key to ascending and truly transforming your life. Surrender in each moment as it comes, and you will live a life full of rich moments." (Author Unknown)

This meditation starts with a body scan that assists in relaxation and focus and leads into the portion specific on To Be Still and Listen.

• *Body Scan*

Now close your eyes, leave all your worries at the door. Allow yourself to relax into the moment. There is only right here, right now.

Clinging to nothing, just be at rest with what is.
(pause)

Focus on your breathing and the words you hear and if your mind gets distracted, let my voice bring you back and then focus again on your breathing.

Relax now and just breathe.
(pause)

Observe the natural rhythm and flow of your breath.

Take a few moments now, to pay closer attention to it, giving thanks for its presence.
(pause)

Notice the pause at the top of your inhale and again at the bottom of your exhale.
(pause)

Go within, don't think, just breathe.
(pause)

Take a long slow deep breath in and hold it for a moment. Then slowly exhale with a sigh. Allow any tension to melt away.
(pause)

Feel the coolness of the air on the tip of your nose as you inhale and the warmth of the breath as you exhale.
(pause)

Feel the rise of your chest and abdomen on each inhale and the fall on every exhale. As you exhale, let go of any stress or tension, see it floating away, as you gradually relax more deeply with each breath.
(pause)

Grounding ourselves helps us to shed any feelings of anxiety, restlessness, or fear that may be lingering in body or mind.

So, take a few minutes now to feel grounded and simply connected to the earth. Notice the breath as it nourishes every cell of your body.

(pause)

Focused breathing allows your mind to slow down. On your own really focus on your next three breathes as you gently inhale and exhale.

(pause)

Feel the energy that comes from the earth, its strength and stability. Let this energy ground you. Feel that energy come through the souls of your feet, like a breeze flowing through and over your entire body.

(pause)

Now, feeling that grounded energy, begin to feel a tingle in the tips of your toes and the souls of your feet, know that you are safe, stable, supported and loved.

(pause)

Now, gently bring your focus to your ankles, your calves, your thighs, feeling those muscles relax, as you feel yourself sinking into the surface you are resting upon.

(pause)

Breathe in and breathe out.

Move your focus to your buttocks… and hips, release any tension you may be feeling and allow yourself to drift into a state of deep relaxation.

(pause)

Focus on the base of your spine, relaxing the muscles in your lower back, feel a warmth and think of the strong color red, as this area represents stability, safety, and security.
(pause)

Now allow that feeling of warmth and relaxation to move to your lower abdominal muscles, just below your belly button, and think of the warm color orange, as this area represents creativity and sexual energies.
(pause)

Feel your body relaxing with each breath you take.
(pause)

Move your focus to your upper abdominal muscles, just above your belly button, relax those muscles and feel a warmth and relaxation as you think of the vibrant color yellow, as this area represents will-power, self-esteem, pleasure, and personal responsibility.
(pause)

Breathe in God's love and peace and breathe out all resistance.
(pause)

Now feel the warmth and relaxation move slowly and gently to your heart center, in the middle of your chest and about two inches in, and think of a beautiful color of green, as this area represents self-love, our love for others and governs our relationships.
(pause)

Feel yourself becoming deeper and deeper relaxed, your breath will assist you.
(pause)

Feel the muscles in your upper back and chest release and open. Relax your neck and shoulders and allow the relaxation to flow through your arms, and hands.

Begin to feel a tingle in your fingertips and allow any remaining tension in your body to flow out through your fingertips and be released into nothingness.
(pause)

Slowly move your focus to your throat, feeling the muscles of your throat loosen and open, as you think of the soft color of light blue, as this area represents the ability to speak clearly and effectively.

Unclench your teeth, release your jaw muscles, relax the muscles in your cheeks, and just breathe.
(pause)

Let your focus move to your eyes. Now, relax your eye lids and your eye sockets.
(pause)

Gently, move your focus to the spot near the middle of your forehead, between your eyebrows. Relax your eyebrows and all the muscles in your forehead, and think of the color indigo blue, as this area represents foresight, intuition, clarity, and is driven by openness and imagination.

(pause)

Bring your focus to the very top of your head, the crown of your head, feel a tingle there as you relax the muscles in your scalp, and feel it opening as you think of the majestic color of purple, as this area represents Divine connection, and a higher state of consciousness.

(pause)

Now, imagine a bright and beautiful ribbon of crystalline white light coming from above and tethering you to the heavens. Let that light flow to you and through you, enveloping you in a bubble of love and protection.

(pause)

Take a deep breath in and as you exhale allow any remaining tension to be released from your body. Repeating these words in your mind, "peace begins within, peace begins within."

(pause)

Just breathe and softly go within.

(pause)

• *Guided Meditation*

Release anything weighing heavy upon your mind or heart.

Be willing and ask your Higher Power to take it and see it float away, feel the lightness in your body and soul.
(pause)

Breathe in and breathe out, concentrate on your breathing, the natural rhythm of your breath. You are starting a new life, with a new sense of hope.

To have this new life, pause and be still, and make a conscience contact with your Higher Power. God loves you and is always with you, just waiting for you to reach out.
(pause)

You need willingness to reach out to your Higher Power and ask for help.

Just Breathe.
(pause)

Now feel this beautiful pure light of God's love come into you, into your mind, into your body and into your spirit. Feel the warmth and peace with each breath you take. Just be still and feel this in every cell of your body, this unconditional love of your Higher Power.
(pause)

Ask your Higher Power, what is my next right step and help me to take it? Then be willing to listen with your heart.

(pause)

Do you have something weighing heavy on your heart? Is something holding you back? Drop that thing that is pulling you down and give it to The Maker of the Universe. In this quiet, peaceful, and safe place inside of you, share your concern with your Higher Power and ask your Higher Power for guidance…Be willing to listen and then be still.

(pause)

Just Breathe.

(pause)

A word or words, perhaps images come into your mind now, these are from your Higher Power. Let yourself receive these, and then pause and let them resonate inside of you.

(pause)

Your Higher Power has infinite wisdom, and this is how you tune in and tap in, to that source of love, guidance, and wisdom.

(pause)

Your Higher Power loves you and wants you to love yourself and others. God wants you to be happy, joyous, and free.

(pause)

Again, ask your Higher Power for help in any area of your life in which you are struggling and after you ask God for help, say, "I am willing to listen for your answer" then be still.

(pause)

Continue to breathe in and breathe out, relax, and feel the presence of unconditional love, don't try to force anything, just feel the peace within.

(pause)

As you relax and breathe, take note of feelings, words, or images.

(pause)

Your Higher Power has perfect timing and sometimes the answer might be, to do nothing and just wait. Trust God... let go of control....

(pause)

Relax and just be.

(pause)

Do you need to ask your Divine Spirit for help in any of these areas...for serenity or acceptance, for courage or wisdom, to take away a character flaw, to remember to pause when agitated, to give forgiveness, for honesty or humility, maybe, how to be in harmony with your fellow man?

Perhaps you need to ask God to help you to be willing to be willing?

Do that now.
(pause)

Hear this prayer, "God, direct my thoughts and actions today so that I am humble and honest, walking in your will, mindful of others and a walking example of love."

Pause for a moment and let that prayer soak in.

Breathe in and breathe out.
(pause)

• *Closing*

Start to deepen your breath now and become more aware of your physical body. Take a deep breath in and release it with a sigh. Start to wiggle your fingers and toes, stretch your arms and legs, open your eyes, and come back to the present time and space.

NAMASTE'

Meditation for Using Your Breath to Let Go

Surrender is the key to ascending and truly transforming your life. Surrender in each moment as it comes, and you will live a life full of rich moments. (Author Unknown)

This meditation starts with a body scan that assists in relaxation and focus and leads into the portion specific on Using Your Breath to Let Go.

• *Body Scan*

Now close your eyes, leave all your worries at the door. Allow yourself to relax into the moment. There is only right here, right now.

Clinging to nothing, just be at rest with what is.
(pause)

Focus on your breathing and the words you hear and if your mind gets distracted, let my voice bring you back and then focus again on your breathing.

Relax now and just breathe.
(pause)

Observe the natural rhythm and flow of your breath.

Take a few moments now, to pay closer attention to it, giving thanks for its presence.
(pause)

Notice the pause at the top of your inhale and again at the bottom of your exhale.
(pause)

Go within, don't think, just breathe.
(pause)

Take a long slow deep breath in and hold it for a moment. Then slowly exhale with a sigh. Allow any tension to melt away.
(pause)

Feel the coolness of the air on the tip of your nose as you inhale and the warmth of the breath as you exhale.
(pause)

Feel the rise of your chest and abdomen on each inhale and the fall on every exhale. As you exhale, let go of any stress or tension, see it floating away, as you gradually relax more deeply with each breath.
(pause)

Grounding ourselves helps us to shed any feelings of anxiety, restlessness, or fear that may be lingering in body or mind.

So, take a few minutes now to feel grounded and simply connected to the earth. Notice the breath as it nourishes every cell of your body.

(pause)

Focused breathing allows your mind to slow down. On your own really focus on your next three breathes as you gently inhale and exhale.

(pause)

Feel the energy that comes from the earth, its strength and stability. Let this energy ground you. Feel that energy come through the souls of your feet, like a breeze flowing through and over your entire body.

(pause)

Now, feeling that grounded energy, begin to feel a tingle in the tips of your toes and the souls of your feet, know that you are safe, stable, supported and loved.

(pause)

Now, gently bring your focus to your ankles, your calves, your thighs, feeling those muscles relax, as you feel yourself sinking into the surface you are resting upon.

(pause)

Breathe in and breathe out.

Move your focus to your buttocks… and hips, release any tension you may be feeling and allow yourself to drift into a state of deep relaxation.

(pause)

Focus on the base of your spine, relaxing the muscles in your lower back, feel a warmth and think of the strong color red, as this area represents stability, safety, and security.

(pause)

Now allow that feeling of warmth and relaxation to move to your lower abdominal muscles, just below your belly button, and think of the warm color orange, as this area represents creativity and sexual energies.

(pause)

Feel your body relaxing with each breath you take.

(pause)

Move your focus to your upper abdominal muscles, just above your belly button, relax those muscles and feel a warmth and relaxation as you think of the vibrant color yellow, as this area represents will-power, self-esteem, pleasure, and personal responsibility.

(pause)

Breathe in God's love and peace and breathe out all resistance.

(pause)

Now feel the warmth and relaxation move slowly and gently to your heart center, in the middle of your chest and about two inches in, and think of a beautiful color of green, as this area represents self-love, our love for others and governs our relationships.

(pause)

Feel yourself becoming deeper and deeper relaxed, your breath will assist you.

(pause)

Feel the muscles in your upper back and chest release and open. Relax your neck and shoulders and allow the relaxation to flow through your arms, and hands.

Begin to feel a tingle in your fingertips and allow any remaining tension in your body to flow out through your fingertips and be released into nothingness.

(pause)

Slowly move your focus to your throat, feeling the muscles of your throat loosen and open, as you think of the soft color of light blue, as this area represents the ability to speak clearly and effectively.

Unclench your teeth, release your jaw muscles, relax the muscles in your cheeks, and just breathe.

(pause)

Let your focus move to your eyes. Now, relax your eye lids and your eye sockets.

(pause)

Gently, move your focus to the spot near the middle of your forehead, between your eyebrows. Relax your eyebrows and all the muscles in your forehead, and think of the color indigo blue, as this area represents foresight, intuition, clarity, and is driven by openness and imagination.

(pause)

Bring your focus to the very top of your head, the crown of your head, feel a tingle there as you relax the muscles in your scalp, and feel it opening as you think of the majestic color of purple, as this area represents Divine connection, and a higher state of consciousness.
(pause)

Now, imagine a bright and beautiful ribbon of crystalline white light coming from above and tethering you to the heavens. Let that light flow to you and through you, enveloping you in a bubble of love and protection.
(pause)

Take a deep breath in and as you exhale allow any remaining tension to be released from your body. Repeating these words in your mind, "peace begins within, peace begins within."
(pause)

Just breathe and softly go within.
(pause)

• *Guided Meditation*

Focus on the breath, let it soften…feel your body soften.
(pause)

See and feel that warm, soft, sweet, and beautiful ribbon of crystalline white light coming from above. It is a light of love and peace.
(pause)

Resting in your breath, resting in love, feel yourself relaxing and becoming a bit softer.

Each breath, gentle, soft, and sweet.
(pause)

Feel the rise and fall of each breath, slow and easy.

As you rest in your breath, release all resistance, and feel any sharp edges melting and becoming soft.
(pause)

Relax.
(pause)

Cling to nothing, feel the light and love fill your body as you focus on your breath.
(pause)

Become aware of the peace within you.
(pause)

Feel the warmth of love as it easily flows to you and through you.
(pause)

See and feel yourself enveloped by a cloud of loving sparkling gold and silver crystalline light.
(pause)

Safe, sweet, soft, surrender.
(pause)

Relax, let your breath be gentle and feel safe and protected.
(pause)

Feel the presence of unconditional love.
(pause)

Feel yourself letting go of any negativity, guilt, judgement, or anger lingering within you.
(pause)

It all melts away as you give it to your Higher Power.
(pause)

Feel the lightness of your heart center and let the warm, soft, liquid radiance of love fill you to overflowing.
(pause)

Now, just breathe.
(pause)

Be completely in this moment, right here, right now.
(pause)

Resting in your breath.
(pause)

The gentle rise and fall of your chest.
(pause)

Letting go and letting God.
(pause)

Feel the peace within you.
(pause)

Really focus and imprint a memory of how you feel in this quiet place within you.
(pause)

Repeat to yourself, "Peace begins within."
(pause)

Again, rest in your breath.
(pause)

Relax.
(pause)

Each breath soft, sweet, warm.
(pause)

This peace is always available to you.
(pause)

Let the light of love shine from within you.
(pause)

Let it shine in your smile.
(pause)

Let it shine in your eyes.
(pause)

Let it shine in your words and in your actions.
(pause)

Be that safe, loving, gentle light.
(pause)

Feel it grow inside you, in your heart center as it becomes a part of the core of who you truly are.
(pause)

Deep inside your inner being, it feels right and good.
(pause)

Gently, bring your focus back to the breath, breathing in and out.
(pause)

• *Closing*

Start to deepen your breath now and become more aware of your physical body. Take a deep breath in and release it with a sigh. Start to wiggle your fingers and toes, stretch your arms and legs, open your eyes, and come back to the present time and space.

NAMASTE'

Meditation for "The Serenity Prayer"

"Surrender is the key to ascending and truly transforming your life. Surrender in each moment as it comes, and you will live a life full of rich moments." (Author Unknown)

This meditation starts with a body scan that assists in relaxation and focus and leads into the portion specific on The Serenity Prayer.

• *Body Scan*

Now close your eyes, leave all your worries at the door. Allow yourself to relax into the moment. There is only right here, right now.

Clinging to nothing, just be at rest with what is.
(pause)

Focus on your breathing and the words you hear and if your mind gets distracted, let my voice bring you back and then focus again on your breathing.

Relax now and just breathe.
(pause)

Observe the natural rhythm and flow of your breath.

Take a few moments now, to pay closer attention to it, giving thanks for its presence.
(pause)

Notice the pause at the top of your inhale and again at the bottom of your exhale.
(pause)

Go within, don't think, just breathe.
(pause)

Take a long slow deep breath in and hold it for a moment. Then slowly exhale with a sigh. Allow any tension to melt away.
(pause)

Feel the coolness of the air on the tip of your nose as you inhale and the warmth of the breath as you exhale.
(pause)

Feel the rise of your chest and abdomen on each inhale and the fall on every exhale. As you exhale, let go of any stress or tension, see it floating away, as you gradually relax more deeply with each breath.
(pause)

Grounding ourselves helps us to shed any feelings of anxiety, restlessness, or fear that may be lingering in body or mind.

So, take a few minutes now to feel grounded and simply connected to the earth. Notice the breath as it nourishes every cell of your body.

(pause)

Focused breathing allows your mind to slow down. On your own really focus on your next three breathes as you gently inhale and exhale.

(pause)

Feel the energy that comes from the earth, its strength and stability. Let this energy ground you. Feel that energy come through the souls of your feet, like a breeze flowing through and over your entire body.

(pause)

Now, feeling that grounded energy, begin to feel a tingle in the tips of your toes and the souls of your feet, know that you are safe, stable, supported and loved.

(pause)

Now, gently bring your focus to your ankles, your calves, your thighs, feeling those muscles relax, as you feel yourself sinking into the surface you are resting upon.

(pause)

Breathe in and breathe out.

Move your focus to your buttocks… and hips, release any tension you may be feeling and allow yourself to drift into a state of deep relaxation.

(pause)

Focus on the base of your spine, relaxing the muscles in your lower back, feel a warmth and think of the strong color red, as this area represents stability, safety, and security.
(pause)

Now allow that feeling of warmth and relaxation to move to your lower abdominal muscles, just below your belly button, and think of the warm color orange, as this area represents creativity and sexual energies.
(pause)

Feel your body relaxing with each breath you take.
(pause)

Move your focus to your upper abdominal muscles, just above your belly button, relax those muscles and feel a warmth and relaxation as you think of the vibrant color yellow, as this area represents will-power, self-esteem, pleasure, and personal responsibility.
(pause)

Breathe in God's love and peace and breathe out all resistance.
(pause)

Now feel the warmth and relaxation move slowly and gently to your heart center, in the middle of your chest and about two inches in, and think of a beautiful color of green, as this area represents self-love, our love for others and governs our relationships.
(pause)

Feel yourself becoming deeper and deeper relaxed, your breath will assist you.

(pause)

Feel the muscles in your upper back and chest release and open. Relax your neck and shoulders and allow the relaxation to flow through your arms, and hands.

Begin to feel a tingle in your fingertips and allow any remaining tension in your body to flow out through your fingertips and be released into nothingness.

(pause)

Slowly move your focus to your throat, feeling the muscles of your throat loosen and open, as you think of the soft color of light blue, as this area represents the ability to speak clearly and effectively.

Unclench your teeth, release your jaw muscles, relax the muscles in your cheeks, and just breathe.

(pause)

Let your focus move to your eyes. Now, relax your eye lids and your eye sockets.

(pause)

Gently, move your focus to the spot near the middle of your forehead, between your eyebrows. Relax your eyebrows and all the muscles in your forehead, and think of the color indigo blue, as this area represents foresight, intuition, clarity, and is driven by openness and imagination.

(pause)

Bring your focus to the very top of your head, the crown of your head, feel a tingle there as you relax the muscles in your scalp, and feel it opening as you think of the majestic color of purple, as this area represents Divine connection, and a higher state of consciousness.
(pause)

Now, imagine a bright and beautiful ribbon of crystalline white light coming from above and tethering you to the heavens. Let that light flow to you and through you, enveloping you in a bubble of love and protection.
(pause)

Take a deep breath in and as you exhale allow any remaining tension to be released from your body. Repeating these words in your mind, "peace begins within, peace begins within."
(pause)

Just breathe and softly go within.
(pause)

- *Guided Meditation*

Serenity Prayer: "God, grant me the serenity to accept the things I cannot change, the courage to change the things I can, and the wisdom to know the difference."[109]
(pause)

---

[109] Huff, 2007, 12 Step Companion AA Big Book, Version 2.5.9.6., Updated 2020, [Mobile app] Apple/App Store, © 2007 Dean Huff

Relax with each breath you take.
(pause)

What do the words serenity and acceptance mean? Serenity is a quality, or state of being calm and peaceful.[110] Acceptance is to endure without protest or reaction, readiness, or willingness to accept or adapt to a given circumstance.[111]
(pause)

God, grant me a calm and peaceful spirit and to maintain that peacefulness in difficult or unpleasant situations.
(pause)

We have no control or ability to change people, places, and things, yet with God's help, we can have a calm and peaceful spirit in unpleasant situations.
(pause)

Think of an unpleasant situation that you have experienced recently. Did you ask God for help?
(pause)

Emotionally stepping back, pausing, and becoming an observer, your Higher Power can help bring in that serenity, peace, and calmness.
(pause)

---

[110] "Serenity." *Merriam-Webster.com Dictionary*, Merriam-Webster, https://www.merriam-webster.com/dictionary/serenity. Accessed 5 Jul. 2022

[111] "Accept." *Merriam-Webster.com Dictionary*, Merriam-Webster, https://www.merriam-webster.com/dictionary/accept. Accessed 15 Aug. 2022.

In the Serenity Prayer, we ask for courage to change the thing I can. The only thing we can honestly change is ourselves, with the help of a Higher Power.
(pause)

Breathe in and breathe out.
(pause)

So, what is courage?

Courage is mental or moral strength to venture, persevere, and withstand fear or difficulty.[112]
(pause)

The courage we seek in the Serenity Prayer is to have the mental or moral strength to change ourselves, to persevere in doing the work to grow, even when it gets difficult.
(pause)

Think of a recent situation where you showed mental or moral strength, persevered in a difficult situation and displayed courage.
(pause)

Lastly, we seek the wisdom to know the difference in the things we can change, which is only ourselves, and things you cannot change, which is everything else.
(pause)

---

[112] "Courage." *Merriam-Webster.com Dictionary*, Merriam-Webster, https://www.merriam-webster.com/dictionary/courage. Accessed 5 Jul. 2022.

Wisdom is an ability to have insight, good sense in judgement.[113]

(pause)

In difficult situations, if we pause and pray the serenity prayer, we have a better chance of having insight, discernment, and good sense in judgement.

(pause)

The Maker of the Universe is always available to us, and the serenity prayer is a wonderful prayer to use when you just don't know what to do.

(pause)

Remember, peace begins within. So, after you pray, take time to be still and listen.

(pause)

The answers will come if your own house is in order. But obviously you cannot transmit something you haven't got. See to it that your relationship with Him is right, and great events will come to pass for you and countless others. This is the Great Fact for us."[114]

(pause)

Breathe in and breathe out.

(pause)

---

[113] "Wisdom." *Merriam-Webster.com Dictionary*, Merriam-Webster, https://www.merriam-webster.com/dictionary/wisdom. Accessed 5 Jul. 2022.

[114] Alcoholics Anonymous Big Book (4th ed.). (2002). Alcoholics Anonymous World Services. (Page 164)

In your mind, join me in saying the serenity prayer. "God, grant me the serenity to accept the things I cannot change, the courage to change the things I can and the wisdom to know the difference."[115]
(pause)

Peace begins within.
(pause)

- *Closing*

Start to deepen your breath now and become more aware of your physical body. Take a deep breath in and release it with a sigh. Start to wiggle your fingers and toes, stretch your arms and legs, open your eyes, and come back to the present time and space.

NAMASTE'

---

[115] Huff, 2007, 12 Step Companion AA Big Book, Version 2.5.9.6., Updated 2020, [Mobile app] Apple/App Store, © 2007 Dean Huff

Meditation for Gratitude and Trust

"Surrender is the key to ascending and truly transforming your life. Surrender in each moment as it comes, and you will live a life full of rich moments." (Author Unknown)

This meditation starts with a body scan that assists in relaxation and focus and leads into the portion specific on Gratitude and Trust.

- *Body Scan*

Now close your eyes, leave all your worries at the door. Allow yourself to relax into the moment. There is only right here, right now.

Clinging to nothing, just be at rest with what is.
(pause)

Focus on your breathing and the words you hear and if your mind gets distracted, let my voice bring you back and then focus again on your breathing.

Relax now and just breathe.
(pause)

Observe the natural rhythm and flow of your breath.

Take a few moments now, to pay closer attention to it, giving thanks for its presence.
(pause)

Notice the pause at the top of your inhale and again at the bottom of your exhale.
(pause)

Go within, don't think, just breathe.
(pause)

Take a long slow deep breath in and hold it for a moment. Then slowly exhale with a sigh. Allow any tension to melt away.
(pause)

Feel the coolness of the air on the tip of your nose as you inhale and the warmth of the breath as you exhale.
(pause)

Feel the rise of your chest and abdomen on each inhale and the fall on every exhale. As you exhale, let go of any stress or tension, see it floating away, as you gradually relax more deeply with each breath.
(pause)

Grounding ourselves helps us to shed any feelings of anxiety, restlessness, or fear that may be lingering in body or mind.

So, take a few minutes now to feel grounded and simply connected to the earth. Notice the breath as it nourishes every cell of your body.

(pause)

Focused breathing allows your mind to slow down. On your own really focus on your next three breathes as you gently inhale and exhale.

(pause)

Feel the energy that comes from the earth, its strength and stability. Let this energy ground you. Feel that energy come through the souls of your feet, like a breeze flowing through and over your entire body.

(pause)

Now, feeling that grounded energy, begin to feel a tingle in the tips of your toes and the souls of your feet, know that you are safe, stable, supported and loved.

(pause)

Now, gently bring your focus to your ankles, your calves, your thighs, feeling those muscles relax, as you feel yourself sinking into the surface you are resting upon.

(pause)

Breathe in and breathe out.

Move your focus to your buttocks… and hips, release any tension you may be feeling and allow yourself to drift into a state of deep relaxation.

(pause)

Focus on the base of your spine, relaxing the muscles in your lower back, feel a warmth and think of the strong color red, as this area represents stability, safety, and security.
(pause)

Now allow that feeling of warmth and relaxation to move to your lower abdominal muscles, just below your belly button, and think of the warm color orange, as this area represents creativity and sexual energies.
(pause)

Feel your body relaxing with each breath you take.
(pause)

Move your focus to your upper abdominal muscles just above your belly button, relax those muscles and feel a warmth and relaxation as you think of the vibrant color yellow, as this area represents will-power, self-esteem, pleasure, and personal responsibility.
(pause)

Breathe in God's love and peace and breathe out all resistance.
(pause)

Now feel the warmth and relaxation move slowly and gently to your heart center, in the middle of your chest and about two inches in, and think of a beautiful color of green, as this area represents self-love, our love for others and governs our relationships.
(pause)

Feel yourself becoming deeper and deeper relaxed, your breath will assist you.
(pause)

Feel the muscles in your upper back and chest release and open. Relax your neck and shoulders and allow the relaxation to flow through your arms, and hands.

Begin to feel a tingle in your fingertips and allow any remaining tension in your body to flow out through your fingertips and be released into nothingness.
(pause)

Slowly move your focus to your throat, feeling the muscles of your throat loosen and open, as you think of the soft color of light blue, as this area represents the ability to speak clearly and effectively.

Unclench your teeth, release your jaw muscles, relax the muscles in your cheeks, and just breathe.
(pause)

Let your focus move to your eyes. Now, relax your eye lids and your eye sockets.
(pause)

Gently, move your focus to the spot near the middle of your forehead, between your eyebrows. Relax your eyebrows and all the muscles in your forehead, and think of the color indigo blue, as this area represents foresight, intuition, clarity, and is driven by openness and imagination.
(pause)

Bring your focus to the very top of your head, the crown of your head, feel a tingle there as you relax the muscles in your scalp, and feel it opening as you think of the majestic color of purple, as this area represents Divine connection, and a higher state of consciousness.
(pause)

Now, imagine a bright and beautiful ribbon of crystalline white light coming from above and tethering you to the heavens. Let that light flow to you and through you, enveloping you in a bubble of love and protection.
(pause)

Take a deep breath in and as you exhale allow any remaining tension to be released from your body. Repeating these words in your mind, "peace begins within, peace begins within."
(pause)

• *Guided Meditation*

You are creating a new life and a new way of living.
(pause)

You have the strength and power to achieve anything. Allow yourself to be excited about the life you are creating.
(pause)

Fulfillment, joy, acceptance, love, trust, and gratitude are found not in things but within your heart and soul.
(pause)

Ego can get in the way of gratitude; acceptance makes gratitude flow.

(pause)

You are on a path of healing. Believe in yourself and trust yourself.

(pause)

You have access to the Creator of the Universe, Source Energy, God, your Higher Power. Feel the frequency of gratitude. Feel your physical body clear, cleanse, and release any struggle. Your breath will assist you.

(pause)

Trust that you are doing your best. Trust that you can overcome fear, worry, doubt and guilt. You get to choose, experience, allow, accept, and take action as you heal and grow into your new way of living.

(pause)

You are free and you are powerful. Plant seeds of positive change and let go of the things that no longer serve you.

(pause)

Relax and go within.

(pause)

Trust that everything is working out for you. Trust that your needs will be provided for.

Say, thank you, thank you, thank you.
(pause)

You are now able to see that challenges are opportunities to grow and to learn. Some of your greatest lessons become your greatest blessings.
(pause)

Tap into your Divine Spirit. Accept the assistance, feel the calm, relax and just be.
(pause)

Feel serenity grow inside you. Allow it to spread throughout your entire body.
(pause)

Say, thank you and feel the peace and gratitude in your heart center.
(pause)

Know you are exactly where you need to be, right here, right now.
(pause)

The momentum of your growth is found in stillness. In the stillness, let go of fear and doubt and trust your Higher Power. Let go, and let your life unfold.
(pause)

Feel liberation, joy, trust, gratitude, love, and acceptance as these feelings align you with the source of all that is good and true, the God of your understanding.
(pause)

Be in the present moment, you are okay, right here, right now. Be kind to yourself and feel love for yourself.
(pause)

Trust and know that your Higher Power, your Divine Spirit is with you always.
(pause)

The God of your understanding cannot help if you do not seek and ask for help. Ask your Divine Spirit to give you nudges and divine inspiration. Then be still and listen to the whispers of God. Listen with your heart.
(pause)

Feel gratitude and trust as you visualize yourself with everything working out for your higher good. Relax and breathe in the love of your Higher Power, feel it in the depth of your soul.
(pause)

See the beauty, feel the peace within.
(pause)

Relax now and just feel the natural rhythm of your breath.

• *Closing*

Start to deepen your breath now and become more aware of your physical body. Take a deep breath in and release it with a sigh. Start to wiggle your fingers and toes, stretch your arms and legs, open your eyes, and come back to the present time and space.

NAMASTE'

Meditation for Living in the Present Moment

"Surrender is the key to ascending and truly transforming your life. Surrender in each moment as it comes, and you will live a life full of rich moments." (Author Unknown)

This meditation starts with a body scan that assists in relaxation and focus and leads into the portion specific on Living in the Present Moment.

- ### *Body Scan*

Now close your eyes, leave all your worries at the door. Allow yourself to relax into the moment. There is only right here, right now.

Clinging to nothing, just be at rest with what is.
(pause)

Focus on your breathing and the words you hear and if your mind gets distracted, let my voice bring you back and then focus again on your breathing.

Relax now and just breathe.
(pause)

Observe the natural rhythm and flow of your breath.

Take a few moments now, to pay closer attention to it, giving thanks for its presence.
(pause)

Notice the pause at the top of your inhale and again at the bottom of your exhale.
(pause)

Go within, don't think, just breathe.
(pause)

Take a long slow deep breath in and hold it for a moment. Then slowly exhale with a sigh. Allow any tension to melt away.
(pause)

Feel the coolness of the air on the tip of your nose as you inhale and the warmth of the breath as you exhale.
(pause)

Feel the rise of your chest and abdomen on each inhale and the fall on every exhale. As you exhale, let go of any stress or tension, see it floating away, as you gradually relax more deeply with each breath.
(pause)

Grounding ourselves helps us to shed any feelings of anxiety, restlessness, or fear that may be lingering in body or mind.

So, take a few minutes now to feel grounded and simply connected to the earth. Notice the breath as it nourishes every cell of your body.

(pause)

Focused breathing allows your mind to slow down. On your own really focus on your next three breathes as you gently inhale and exhale.

(pause)

Feel the energy that comes from the earth, its strength and stability. Let this energy ground you. Feel that energy come through the souls of your feet, like a breeze flowing through and over your entire body.

(pause)

Now, feeling that grounded energy, begin to feel a tingle in the tips of your toes and the souls of your feet, know that you are safe, stable, supported and loved.

(pause)

Now, gently bring your focus to your ankles, your calves, your thighs, feeling those muscles relax, as you feel yourself sinking into the surface you are resting upon.

(pause)

Breathe in and breathe out.

Move your focus to your buttocks… and hips, release any tension you may be feeling and allow yourself to drift into a state of deep relaxation.

(pause)

Focus on the base of your spine, relaxing the muscles in your lower back, feel a warmth and think of the strong color red, as this area represents stability, safety, and security.
(pause)

Now allow that feeling of warmth and relaxation to move to your lower abdominal muscles, just below your belly button, and think of the warm color orange, as this area represents creativity and sexual energies.
(pause)

Feel your body relaxing with each breath you take.
(pause)

Move your focus to your upper abdominal muscles just above your belly button, relax those muscles and feel a warmth and relaxation as you think of the vibrant color yellow, as this area represents will-power, self-esteem, pleasure, and personal responsibility.
(pause)

Breathe in God's love and peace and breathe out all resistance.
(pause)

Now feel the warmth and relaxation move slowly and gently to your heart center, in the middle of your chest and about two inches in, and think of a beautiful color of green, as this area represents self-love, our love for others and governs our relationships.
(pause)

Feel yourself becoming deeper and deeper relaxed, your breath will assist you.

(pause)

Feel the muscles in your upper back and chest release and open. Relax your neck and shoulders and allow the relaxation to flow through your arms, and hands.

Begin to feel a tingle in your fingertips and allow any remaining tension in your body to flow out through your fingertips and be released into nothingness.

(pause)

Slowly move your focus to your throat, feeling the muscles of your throat loosen and open, as you think of the soft color of light blue, as this area represents the ability to speak clearly and effectively.

Unclench your teeth, release your jaw muscles, relax the muscles in your cheeks, and just breathe.

(pause)

Let your focus move to your eyes. Now, relax your eye lids and your eye sockets.

(pause)

Gently, move your focus to the spot near the middle of your forehead, between your eyebrows. Relax your eyebrows and all the muscles in your forehead, and think of the color indigo blue, as this area represents foresight, intuition, clarity, and is driven by openness and imagination.

(pause)

Bring your focus to the very top of your head, the crown of your head, feel a tingle there as you relax the muscles in your scalp, and feel it opening as you think of the majestic color of purple, as this area represents Divine connection, and a higher state of consciousness.

(pause)

Now, imagine a bright and beautiful ribbon of crystalline white light coming from above and tethering you to the heavens. Let that light flow to you and through you, enveloping you in a bubble of love and protection.

(pause)

Take a deep breath in and as you exhale allow any remaining tension to be released from your body. Repeating these words in your mind, "peace begins within, peace begins within."

(pause)

• *Guided Meditation*

Soothing feelings of relaxation flow within you. Feel the lightness in your body and soul.

(pause)

Your body feels balanced and centered. You are comfortable, peaceful, and relaxed. No thoughts of the past, no thoughts of the future, only the present moment.

(pause)

Imagine that you are flying, soaring with the eagles. You turn to one and ask, "What time is it?" The eagle replies, "It's now!"[116] You realize that man made up time and that God and nature did not.

(pause)

At this moment from the view high above, imagine, you have a view of the past, present, and future. Your view reminds you that you do not live in the past, and you do not live in the future. You realize that where you truly live is right here, right now and in each and every moment.

(pause)

You can feel the truth and knowledge that your soul is joyful, peaceful, and grateful in this now moment.

(pause)

From this vantage point, you can observe the past, learn from the past and grow, knowing you do not live there. As you observer, you recognize that you are not emotionally connected to what you are watching, you are simply observing.

(pause)

Right here, right now, you awaken to the knowledge that this view and your ability to observe is a beautiful tool to use to grow, and to be the person, to be the soul, you were born to be.

(pause)

---

[116] Tolle, E. (2004). *The power of now: A guide to spiritual enlightenment.* (Page 34)

Your soul has wisdom to observe any lesson from the past that is relevant and apply those lessons in your present life.
(pause)

Breathe in God's peace and exhale resistance.
(pause)

Again, from this view, soring high above, you try to focus on the future, however, it is out of focus, you see a blurry mist, full of beautiful colors and you feel pleasure and joy. However, you know you do not live there.
(pause)

You can make goals and set intentions, and work towards them. Knowing your focus in the here and now, this present moment, is making your path towards your future.
(pause)

It is essential for you to live in the present moment to grow and apply life lessons.
(pause)

Remember to keep breathing in and breathing out.
(pause)

As you relax in this present moment, you are aware of where you want to go, and you give your full attention to the steps that you are taking.
(pause)

Relax in the thought of now. "One Day at a Time," "One Step at a Time," "One Moment at a Time."
(pause)

Remember, you can change gears and slow down, when necessary, pause, or even start your day all over.
(pause)

You feel joy as you see and smell the flowers by the wayside and are aware of the beauty and the miracle of the life that is unfolding all around you as you are focused on living in the present moment.
(pause)

So, when you see flowers, pause, and smell them, when you observe birds flying in the sky, let it be a reminder to pause and be fully present in your life, in the moment.
(pause)

Take time to do what makes your soul happy, pause and enjoy the moment. All you really have is right here, right now.
(pause)

Remember the tool of learning from the past and applying it in the present.
(pause)

Your future has limitless possibilities.
(pause)

Breathe in peace and love and exhale all resistance.
(pause)

Peace begins within and you have a choice each day to set an intention and focus on being fully in the moment. Today is a good day to have a good day!
(pause)

Silently, repeat these words in your mind: Peace begins within, peace begins within.
(pause)

As you move into each unfolding day, remember this peaceful place you have cultivated within yourself. In any moment, you can return to this place through mindful awareness of the present moment, using your breath and through the stillness that lives within you.
(pause)

• *Closing*

Start to deepen your breath now and become more aware of your physical body. Take a deep breath in and release it with a sigh. Start to wiggle your fingers and toes, stretch your arms and legs, open your eyes, and come back to the present time and space.

NAMASTE'

Lightning Source UK Ltd.
Milton Keynes UK
UKHW010303081222
413533UK00001B/25